MIRACLES *of* MARY

APPARITIONS, LEGENDS, AND MIRACULOUS WORKS
OF THE BLESSED VIRGIN MARY

MICHAEL S. DURHAM

⁂

DESIGNED BY CARMILE S. ZAINO

HarperSanFrancisco
A Division of HarperCollins*Publishers*

FACING PAGE: *Johann Eckhard Löffler and Heinrich Löffler, engraving from* Flores Seraphici . . . , *Cologne, 1640–1642, Spencer Collection, New York Public Library.*

PAGE 1: *Serbian-Orthodox, mid-18th century,* Madonna and Child, *Galerija Matice Srpske, Novi Sad, Serbia.*

TITLE PAGE: *Sandro Botticelli (1445–1510),* Madonna of the Magnificat, *Uffizi Gallery.*

FRONT COVER: *Peruvian, 18th century, Collao School,* Virgin of the Assumption, *private collection, Venice.*

MIRACLES OF MARY: APPARITIONS, LEGENDS, AND MIRACULOUS WORKS OF THE BLESSED VIRGIN MARY

A Blackberry Press Book

Text copyright © 1995 Michael S. Durham
Compilation copyright © 1995 Blackberry Press, Inc., New York.
Additional copyright notices appear on pages 180–186, which constitute an extension of this page.

PROJECT STAFF
Editor: Moira Duggan
Picture research: Gail Reichstein
Additional research: Amy Wilensky, Sloan Seiden, Gail Reichstein
Production consultant: Elizabeth Stoneman
Picture annotations: Lorraine Karafel
Typesetting: Kevin Callahan
Index: Pat Woodruff

1

FIRST EDITION

Library of Congress Cataloguing-in-Publication Data

Durham, Michael S. (Michael Schelling), 1935–
Miracles of Mary : apparitions, legends, and miraculous works of the
blessed Virgin Mary / Michael S. Durham. — 1st ed.
p.   cm.
Includes bibliographical references.
ISBN 0-06-062131-1
1. Mary, Blessed Virgin, Saint—Apparitions and miracles. I. Title.
BT650.D87 1995   95–5093
232.91'7—dc20   CIP

95 96 97 98 99 BBP 10 9 8 7 6 5 4 3 2 1

FVLCITE ME FLO
RIBVS QVIA AMORE
LANGVEO

Contents

Preface

When I am asked if I believe in the miracles and apparitions of the Virgin Mary—or when I find myself pondering this imponderable question—I think of the sixteenth-century saint, Ignatius de Loyola, who, while traveling across Spain, fell into a dispute about Mary with a Moor who argued that she was not a virgin. After they parted, Ignatius was tempted to catch up with the infidel and punish him for his blasphemy, but in the end he left the decision up to his mule. If the animal overtook the Moor, he would punish him. But the mule took another road and Ignatius, a soldier by training, avoided violence.

So it is with me and the miracles and apparitions recounted in this book. True or false? I'm going to let my mule decide. For what matters to me is this: these stories are enchanting, as charming as any tales I know of, be they legend, myth, folk tale, pure fantasy, or fact—or some combination thereof. Taken together, they present a picture of the Virgin Mary in her many guises—to name a few, as healer, builder of churches, dispenser of mercy, intercessor with God, Queen of Peace, repository of world sorrow, and herald of calamities yet to come. To tell these stories as straightforwardly as possible, without bending to the skeptic or to the devout, is the simple purpose of this illustrated book.

This picture of Mary as we know her today is as much a creation of mankind as of scripture. The Mary of the Bible is an indistinct figure. St. Paul, for example, refers to her only obliquely, without naming her. She receives more play in the gospels of Luke and Matthew, but we do not know the details of her life: when she was born, when or where she died, or if, as some believe, she had other children after Jesus. She speaks eloquently in a hymn of praise known as the Magnificat but otherwise she has few lines in the New Testament. It is as if the gospels provide a rough sketch of Mary and we are left to fill in the details.

And so we have; no human in history has so fired the artistic imagination. The Mary who has emerged over two millennia is rich in detail, imagery, and mystery. The sixty illustrations in this book show at least that many aspects of her. She appears as a fresh-faced American child, energetic but determined, in Abbott Handerson Thayer's early-twentieth-century painting. She is a regal figure in a contemporary work from the Philippines and, in Piero della Francesca's masterpiece, an expectant mother, her love so intense it spills over to all mankind. The stories themselves complement the portrait. In the account of Mary's apparition at Guadalupe, Mexico, in 1531 (one of my favorite stories because it shows so many sides of our versatile Mary), she is a complex figure—solicitous, persistent, demanding, and a worker of outstanding miracles.

By its decrees and pronouncements, the Catholic Church also had a hand in rounding out the picture of Mary. In A.D. 381, it declared her perpetual virginity; fifty years later it confirmed her exalted status as the Mother of God; in 1854, it put its imprimatur on the doctrine of the Immaculate Conception, which holds that Mary was conceived in her mother's womb without stain of original sin.

The Church usually proceeds cautiously in its pronouncements about Mary. Theologians were vigorously debating the Immaculate Conception for centuries before it received papal approval. By the Middle Ages, they had formulated the concept, and a painting in a six-

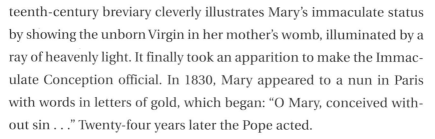

teenth-century breviary cleverly illustrates Mary's immaculate status by showing the unborn Virgin in her mother's womb, illuminated by a ray of heavenly light. It finally took an apparition to make the Immaculate Conception official. In 1830, Mary appeared to a nun in Paris with words in letters of gold, which began: "O Mary, conceived without sin . . ." Twenty-four years later the Pope acted.

For me, a non-Catholic, this is all recently acquired knowledge. The idea for the book came from the book's designer, Carmile Zaino, and it was enthusiastically adopted by Maureen Graney, whose company, Blackberry Press, produced the book. The two women, who had somewhat similar Catholic upbringings and who selected the images that accompany the text, asked me to collaborate with them and to write it.

There was little in my background to prepare me for this assignment. My early religious training was less than rudimentary. I had attended church sporadically, enough to develop an unappealing picture of a God, in the words of a Protestant hymn, "armed with cruel hate." I had heard of the Immaculate Conception, but, like most non-Catholics, I was under the mistaken impression that it had something to do with the birth of Christ.

In 1967, I had a brief exposure to the history of Marian apparitions when I was in Fátima, Portugal, to report on the fiftieth anniversary of her appearance there in 1917, but the experience—marked by huge crowds and the commercialism so common at major shrines—was far from sublime. If I knew Mary at all, it was through art. In my travels, I had seen many of the masterpieces Mary had inspired, some of which are reproduced in this book. But now I wonder: did I comprehend what I was seeing? Without knowing Mary as I know her now—as a loving, ever-perfect mother—and without understanding her sorrow, her suffering, and her exalted status as Mother of God, how could I begin to see what artists saw in Mary or wanted me to see?

There have been reports of Mary appearing on earth her miracles to perform for nearly twenty centuries. Her first recorded appearance was to St. James in Spain in A.D. 40. Since then, by one count, Mary has put in more than twenty thousand separate appearances, and these continue to this day. The year I was at Fátima, Mary was appearing to children in Garabandal, Spain, in a long series of apparitions. Accounts of present-day apparitions at Medjugorje (Bosnia and Herzegovina) and in Queens, New York, are also among the sixty miracles recounted in this book.

Few twentieth-century Marian apparitions are sanctioned by the Catholic Church. Fátima has been approved but Garabandal has not. Nor has Medjugorje, but lack of sanction has not stopped it from becoming one of the world's major Marian shrines. Church approval does not obligate Catholics to believe in an apparition; it only means that they are free to venerate Mary at the place where the apparition occurred. In the eyes of the Church, Mary does perform miracles, but not by her own power. She mediates, or channels, the power that emanates from God.

Mary's role, then, in miracles is one of intermediary or intercessor or mediator in invoking the power of God. She performs this role in the stories throughout the book, but it is best illustrated in Chapter 9, Lady of Legend. In a number of these tales, Mary acts as an advocate for mankind before God. And an effective advocate she is. In one bizarre story, she successfully obtains salvation for a cannibal, whose seventy-eight victims included his wife and two children. Her argument before God: the cannibal had once shown kindness to a beggar "in Mary's name."

The story, as incredible as it is, makes two important points: God is unable to say no to Mary, His Mother; and second, in return for a bare minimum of veneration, Mary will go to bat for you, no matter what your faults. I find that comforting; we all need someone like Mary on our side. For me, she is like a book that has been in my library for years but whose pages I have just recently opened and, with great joy, begun to read.

Lady of Peace and Prayer

O A WAR-STRICKEN WORLD, in which neither politics nor military force is able to end the fighting, a promise by Mary of peace through prayer has powerful appeal. When Mary appeared in 1871 in Pontmain, France, the village, which had sent most of its young men off to war, was being threatened by the Prussian advance. Mary's message there was unequivocal: it took the form of an exhortation—"But pray, my children"—written across the tableau in which she appeared. The impact of the vision was enhanced when France and Prussia declared an armistice soon thereafter.

At Beauraing, Belgium, six years before the outbreak of World War II, the Virgin's words were even more to the point: "Pray always," she told the young children who saw her in a schoolyard garden. Similarly, in Nicaragua in 1980, Mary told Bernardo Martínez, "I want the rosary prayed every day, not just in the month of May but all the time." Implicit in the message was the promise that prayer would end the civil strife that was devastating the country. Mary's apparitions at Medjugorje in Bosnia and Herzegovina began in 1981 and continue to this day. Here Mary identified herself as Gospa, Queen of Peace, and informed the seers that prayer would bring the civil war and ethnic conflict to an end. That has not yet happened, but when Mary speaks hope persists.

Abbott Handerson Thayer (1849–1921), The Virgin, *Freer Gallery of Art, Smithsonian Institution.*

"But Pray My Children"
Pontmain, France, 1871

THE YEAR 1871 STARTED BADLY for France. The country was faltering during the final stages of the Franco-Prussian War; Paris was under siege, about to fall to the enemy. In the village of Pontmain, where cannon fire of the advancing Prussians could be heard in the distance, thirty-eight men had been called away to war. In fact, when twelve-year-old Eugène Barbedette looked out of his barn on the evening of January 17 and saw the image of a lady wearing a black veil suspended in the sky, he took it as a sign that one of his older brothers had been killed in combat.

The lady was dressed in a blue robe decorated with golden stars. Her gold sandals were adorned with a rosette of golden ribbons. Over the veil she wore a crown of gold. Her head was framed by three exceptionally bright stars, which the adults who gathered outside the barn during the apparition could see, even though they could not see the lady herself.

Eugène was the first of five children to see the apparition. The second was his younger brother, ten-year-old Joseph, who was working in the barn with him and their father. When their mother, Victoire, arrived, she angrily called her sons "little liars" and pointed out that they were drawing the attention of the neighbors. She soon had a change of heart, however, and even suggested that the vision might be the Blessed Virgin Mary. But when she fetched her glasses from the house—and still could see nothing—she called the boys home for supper.

After the meal, the image was still there. A nun who taught at the village school arrived with two girls, Françoise Richer, eleven, and Jeanne-Marie Lebosse, nine, who said they could see the figure. Another nun among the fast-growing crowd, Sister Marie Edouard, suspected that only children could see the vision, so she sent for the grandson of a neighbor, Eugène Freiteau, six, and he became the fifth person to see the apparition. Finally, a two-year-old child in its mother's arms pointed to the three bright stars and cried out, "Jesus! Jesus!"

As the apparition progressed, it almost doubled in size. While Sister Marie Edouard led the crowd in prayer, an oval frame appeared around the Virgin. Then these words were spelled out, slowly, letter by letter, in a white space that had appeared beneath the Virgin's feet: "Mais

Arroyo Hondo Santero, Our Lady of Sorrows (detail), santos figure, 1830/40, private collection.

priez mes enfants" ("But pray my children"). As the crowd, by now most of the village, continued to pray and sing hymns, two more sentences appeared: "Dieu vous exaucera en peu de temps" ("God will hear you shortly") and, lastly, "Mon fils se laisse toucher" ("My son permits himself to be moved").

The changes in the image of the apparition continued. A small red cross appeared over her heart and a large cross, from which hung a banner emblazoned with Christ's name, in her hand. Small crosses appeared over her shoulders and four candles in holders on the frame were illuminated, apparently by starlight. Finally, while the parish priest led the crowd in prayers, the tableau disappeared in a white cloud that was visible to everyone present. The apparition had lasted three hours.

Believers in the apparition at Pontmain also consider the aftermath to be miraculous. That night, the Prussians, who were about to overrun the nearby town of Laval, halted their advance, and the danger to Pontmain finally ended when an armistice was signed eleven days later. This felicitous event—and many seemingly miraculous occurrences since—have been widely attributed to the intervention of Our Lady of Pontmain. ⤸

LADY IN THE HAWTHORN TREE
BEAURAING, BELGIUM, 1932

THE SMALL, FRENCH-SPEAKING farming town of Beauraing is located in southern Belgium just a few miles from the French border. There, on the evening of November 29, 1932, the Virgin Mary, her feet covered in little clouds, appeared to five schoolchildren near the Sisters of Christian Doctrine Academy where one of them, Gilberte Voisin, aged thirteen, was a pupil. The children raced home and, in a state of high excitement, told their parents what they had seen. But because the children had a reputation for pranks and mischief, no one believed them.

The next day the children saw the apparition again. This convinced one of their parents, Germaine Degeimbre, that someone was playing a trick on them. When the children returned to the school the following day, December 1, she went with them, and, as they were at the door of the Academy fetching Gilberte, Mme. Degeimbre stayed in the school's garden and beat the bushes with a stick

Jacopo Ligozzi (1547–1627), The Beech Tree of the Madonna at La Verna, *drawing, Metropolitan Museum of Art.*

to flush out the prankster. She found nobody, and, as the children walked away from the school, they had several more visions of Mary.

In one of them, Mary appeared to emerge from some shrubs and ascend to heaven. At this point the youngest child, Gilberte Degeimbre (called Little Gilberte to distinguish her from her older friend, Gilberte Voisin), was overcome by excitement and the children took her home. Three of them returned later that evening, and before they reached the gate of the Academy, they fell to their knees and began reciting the rosary. The Virgin appeared beneath a hawthorn tree in the school's garden. She was young, wore a white gown, and radiated "a kind of blue light," they recalled later. When eleven-year-old Albert Voisin asked the apparition if she was the Virgin Mary, she nodded to indicate that she was.

Mary appeared to the children for the next five days, even though the mother superior of the school had locked the gates of the garden to discourage the children—and the crowds that were beginning to accompany them—from coming to the school. On December 2, when Albert asked the apparition what she wanted, the Virgin replied that she wanted the children to "always be good." In an apparition two days later the Virgin indicated that she would like a chapel built there. On December 5, she ignored the children's request for miracles to convince the skeptical.

December 8 was the Feast of the Immaculate Conception, a day on which the Virgin had specifically asked the children to come to the garden. Some fifteen thousand people gathered around the school that day, many of them expecting the Virgin to cure two invalids who were present. When the children fell to their knees at the sight of the apparition, they were simultaneously examined by doctors who prodded them and shined lights in their eyes, but no cures or other miracles took place.

After December 8, the Virgin appeared to the children less frequently. On December 17, she requested that a chapel be built in the garden where the hawthorn tree stood. On December 28, she warned the children that she would soon be appearing to them for the last time, and the next day, as she opened her arms in a gesture of farewell, Fernande Voisin saw her heart of gold.

Mary's last appearance in Beauraing was on January 3, 1933. On that day, she appeared to all the children except Fernande, who was in tears because

Nicolas Poussin (1594–1665), The Assumption of the Virgin (detail), c. 1626, National Gallery of Art, Washington, D.C.

she could not see her. During this appearance, she spoke to each of the four individually; with Little Gilberte and Albert she shared secrets; to Big Gilberte, she promised, "I will convert sinners"; and she told Andrée Degeimbre, "I am the Mother of God, the Queen of Heaven. Pray always." As she vanished from view, she revealed her heart of gold to the four children.

Afterward, the four children went into the convent, leaving the distraught Fernande kneeling outside. Suddenly, accompanied by a loud noise and a ball of fire in the branches of the hawthorn tree, the Virgin appeared to Fernande, asking the child first if she loved her Son and then, "Do you love me?" When Fernande answered yes to both questions, the Virgin told her, "Sacrifice yourself for me."

That same year, 1933, some two million pilgrims visited the site of the apparitions at Beauraing, even though the Bishop of Namur withheld official approval for devotion to Our Lady of Beauraing for another ten years. In 1949, Pope Pius XII himself authorized the devotion. ⊱

THE LADY ON A CLOUD
CUAPA, NICARAGUA, 1980

A STATUE OF MARY THAT GLOWED mysteriously and other strange lights in the church alerted the sexton, Bernardo Martínez, a tailor in Cuapa, Nicaragua, to the possible presence of the Virgin Mary. But when he told others in the village about the lights, they ridiculed him. So he prayed to Mary, asking her, if she was going to make an appearance, please to choose someone else for the honor of seeing her. He had problems enough without being made fun of by his skeptical neighbors, he explained.

Not long afterward, while he was fishing late in the afternoon of May 8, 1980, he heard a clap of thunder. Suddenly a beautiful woman appeared. She was dressed in white and wore a veil bordered with gold. She stood on a cloud that hovered above a small tree growing out of some rocks. At first he thought she was a statue, but when rays of light from her hands reached him, he knew that she was a true vision. When he asked who she was, she answered: "I come from heaven . . . I am the mother of Jesus."

Mary's message to Bernardo came in two parts. The first was a call to prayer: "I want the rosary to be prayed every day," she told him. "Not just in the month of May but all the time, within the family . . . even by children when they are old enough to understand." She added that the rosary should be prayed "at a set hour" when work in the home would not interfere.

The second part of the message was a dire warning about the fate of Nicaragua and the world: "Nicaragua has suffered much but she is threatened with more suffering. . . . Pray my son, pray the rosary for all the world. Tell believers and nonbelievers that the world is threatened by grave dangers. I ask the Lord to appease his justice, but if you don't change, you will hasten the arrival of the Third World War."

For the next two months— June and July—Bernardo and small groups of people from his church returned to the same place on the eighth day, but the Virgin did not appear. Instead she came to Bernardo in his dreams; in one of them she gave him instructions on how to free a young man, wrongly accused of a crime, from jail. On August 8, the river was flooded, so Bernardo was not able to reach the site of the apparition. But the following month, on September 8, Mary appeared to him—again on a cloud—but this time as a beautiful young girl of about eight. Bernardo

pleaded with her to show herself to the others with him so that they would know he was telling the truth. The Virgin responded that it would do no good, for those who did not believe in her would not be convinced even if they were to see her. Before she disappeared, she told him that in October she would appear again on the thirteenth day.

On that day, Bernardo was accompanied by about fifty people. Around three that afternoon, while they were saying the rosary, they saw two large identical rings of light—one on the ground, the other directly above it in the sky. Then, after two lightning flashes, Mary appeared to Bernardo on a cloud. When Bernardo told her that many did not believe, she began to weep. Then she delivered this message: "Pray the rosary; meditate on the mysteries. Listen to the word of God spoken in them. Love one another. Forgive each other. Make peace. Don't ask for peace without making peace; because if you don't make it, it does no good to ask for it."

Mary told Bernardo that she would no longer appear to him at that place and he shouted out, "Don't leave us, my Mother." As the cloud began to take her away, she assured him that she was always with those who believed. Then she disappeared. ✿

GOSPA, QUEEN OF PEACE
MEDJUGORJE, HERZEGOVINA, 1981–PRESENT

IN LATE JUNE 1981, IN A TROUBLED part of eastern Europe known as Herzegovina, the Virgin Mary began appearing to six young Croatians, who ranged in age from ten to seventeen. In the course of her appearances, ongoing to this day, Mary, called "Gospa" (Mother of God) in Croatian, identified herself as the Queen of Peace and communicated to each of them, individually, a number of secrets, which, it is widely believed, contain warnings about the fate of mankind.

Fifteen-year-old Ivanka Ivanković was the first of the Medjugorje visionaries to see Gospa on June 24, 1981, a Wednesday. She was walking with a friend, Marjana Dragicević, sixteen, on the slope of Mount Podbrdo near their village. At about four that afternoon, Ivanka saw, about two or three hundred yards farther up the mountain, a young woman who seemed to be hovering above the ground. She immediately suspected that the figure might be the Virgin Mary, but when she tried to point it out, her companion, without even looking in that direction, responded derisively: "Come on! Would Our Lady appear to *us?*"

When they returned to the spot with a friend later that afternoon the figure was there again, and this time all three saw her. Soon they were joined by three others. Although the figure seemed to be beckoning them, they were afraid to approach her. The apparition lasted about forty-five minutes.

JUNE 25 (THURSDAY): The young people returned to Mount Podbrdo, and again Ivanka was the first to see the vision, which was farther up the mountain than the day before. When the vision beckoned, the youngsters, who could be seen by others in the village, ran up the steep and rocky slope with amazing speed and stopped and kneeled when they were about six feet away from the figure. When ten-year-old Jakov Colo, the youngest of the visionaries, did not kneel, he was thrown by an invisible force into a thornbush, where he remained on his knees.

The young people described the vision as a woman no more than nineteen or twenty years of age, extraordinarily beautiful, wearing a crown of stars and a long silver dress with a white veil. The apparition lasted ten or fifteen minutes, after which the figure blessed the children—"Go in peace with God"—and rose

Workshop of the Master of the Amsterdam Cabinet (1480/90), Virgin of the Apocalypse, *stained glass, Metropolitan Museum of Art.*

into the air and disappeared. The villagers looking on could not see the Virgin, but they were amazed that the young people bore no cuts or bruises from their sprint up the treacherous slope and that the thornbush had left no marks on Jakov.

JUNE 26 (FRIDAY): Word of the apparitions had spread so quickly through the village and surrounding countryside that on the third day between two and three thousand people were on hand to witness the apparition, although only the six young people could actually see her. This day the vision appeared even higher on the mountain. When the youngsters reached the figure, Vicka Ivanković, seventeen, sprinkled holy water on her, saying, "If you are Our Lady, stay with us. If you are not, go away." The figure smiled. Then, when one of the seers asked her who she was, she replied, "I am the Blessed Virgin Mary."

To the question, "Why have you come here and what do you want?" the Virgin answered, "I have come because there are many believers here. I want to be with you to convert and reconcile everyone."

On the fourth day, June 27, several of the youngsters were summoned to be examined by a team of medical doctors. When they were finally returned to the mountain that evening, the visionaries were alarmed because the large crowd unknowingly was pressing in on the Virgin and even stepping on her long veil. (When that happened the Virgin temporarily disappeared.) On the fifth day (June 28), they asked the Lady, "Dear Blessed Virgin, what do you want of these people?" She replied, "That those here who do not see me, believe like the six of you who see me."

The government meanwhile was trying to discourage people from gathering for the apparitions. At that time, Yugoslavia, of which Herzegovina was one of six republics, was a unified country still under Communist control, although the dictator, Marshal Tito, had been dead for a year. The authorities were immediately suspicious of the apparitions; they feared that the large crowds drawn to them would encourage political dissent, particularly a Croatian separatist movement that was active in the region.

Johann Eckhard Löffler and Heinrich Löffler, engraving from Flores Seraphici . . . *(detail), Cologne, 1640–1642, Spencer Collection, New York Public Library.*

In hopes of finding them insane or ailing, police summoned the young people for medical examinations, but the examiners concluded that they were healthy and normal in all respects. On the sixth day, the authorities sent a doctor to the mountain, who asked the visionaries if she could touch the Virgin. When the children relayed this request, the answer was, "There have always been unfaithful Judases. Let her come." But when the doctor touched her, the Virgin disappeared. (The young visionaries also reported touching the figure; in response to a question, Vicka reported, "Yes, I touched her dress. But it resists like metal.")

JUNE 30 (TUESDAY, SEVENTH DAY): On orders from the authorities, two social workers took the young people on a drive through the surrounding countryside with the intention of keeping them away past the time the Virgin usually appeared. At that hour, the seers asked their escorts to stop the car, but the driver refused until she saw a brilliant light coming from the direction of Mount Podbrdo only a few miles away. Once they were out of the car, the youngsters kneeled by the roadside and began to say their usual prayers. Then the Lady appeared to them—but not to the social workers. On this occasion, the visionaries asked her if she would mind if they went to the church instead of the mountain. After hesitating, she answered: "I will not, my angels."

JULY 1 (WEDNESDAY, EIGHTH DAY): The police, who had been unsuccessful in discouraging the crowds that gathered each day, came to the town to take the visionaries into custody so they would not be able to go to the mountainside. To evade them, the young people ran through vineyards toward the church. At the same time, the Franciscan parish priest, Jozo Zovko, who had been skeptical about the apparitions, heard a voice saying, "Come out and protect the children." He opened the door just as the young people arrived on the run. Later in the day, after the priest had hidden them in the rectory, the youngsters again saw the Virgin; it was the first apparition to take place inside a building.

(Father Jozo, who saw the Virgin himself on one occasion when she appeared to the young people without speaking, was later arrested and convicted of charges of spreading "hostile propaganda." He was imprisoned for eighteen months and, on his release, forbidden to return to Medjugorje. Today he operates a charismatic mission about a half hour's drive away from the town.)

From this day on, the Virgin began to appear in a variety of places, including seven more times in the rectory. After one apparition in the rectory, young Jakov gave a priest a note on which he had written the Virgin's words: "There are many who ask my name. I am the Queen of Peace." She also began to appear to individual children in their homes. Inevitably, the crowds following the seers began to bother them, so in January 1982 priests cleared out a storage room in the church, and the apparitions continued there in relative peace for three more years.

There were also a number of unusual occurrences that indicated to the faithful, who could not see the Virgin Mary, that a miracle was taking place at Medjugorje. On August 2, 1981, a crowd of about one hundred and fifty people, as they waited for the Virgin to appear to the children, saw the setting sun spin on its axis, a phenomenon that was repeated with some variations over the next few days. On several other occasions, the word *Mir*, meaning peace in Croatian, appeared in the sky above a large, fifteen-ton cross on nearby Mount Kriezevac. On October 22, 1981, four priests saw the cross that had been erected in 1933 to commemorate the 1900th

Titian (c. 1488–1576), The Virgin with the Rabbit, 1530, Musée du Louvre.

anniversary of the Crucifixion change first into a white column and then into "a statue with the contour of a woman."

In the course of the apparitions, Mary informed the visionaries that each would receive ten secrets, and that after they had received the tenth, she would no longer appear to them regularly. She also told them that she would continue appearing at Medjugorje until a permanent sign, representing one of the ten secrets, was manifested on the mountain. "This sign will be for the atheists," the Virgin said. "You faithful already have signs, and you have become the signs for the atheists."

There is also a warning in the Virgin's message. "Those of you who wait for a sign to believe will have waited too long," the seers reported her saying.

In an interview, Marjana once specified "the most important things" the Virgin talked about. "Most of all she tells me to pray and fast. And she talks to me about the conversion of people. She says to pray hard for peace in the world because the world is not at peace. She says that prayer is everything and without prayer we can do nothing."

The apparitions have not been approved by the Church. One influential believer, the archbishop of Split-Makarska, said in December 1985, "My personal conviction is that the events at Medjugorje are of supernatural inspiration." Other Church leaders have come out against the apparitions. The bishop of Mostar called them a case of "collective hallucination" that had been exploited by local priests, and two commissions comprised of psychologists, theologians, scientists, and ecclesiastics have concluded that nothing miraculous has occurred at Medjugorje. An influential Jesuit said he was skeptical because of the unnecessary repetitiveness of the messages. "Nor can one understand the banality of the language," he added.

But the pilgrims have come anyway—from all over the world and by the millions, disregarding the bloody civil war that broke out here in 1992. They have transformed Medjugorje, once a backward village of two hundred and fifty families, into a major center of Marian devotion, a city of modern hotels, restaurants, and shops.

Mary continues to appear to the visionaries, but only three—Jakov Colo, Ivan Dragicevíc, and Vicka Ivankovíc—have daily apparitions. Ivanka Ivankovíc and Marjana Dragicevíc, both married with children, see the Virgin only about once a year. Marija Pavlovíc lives in Italy, where her visions continue. ✂

Swabia, The Virgin in a Robe Embroidered with Ears of Corn, 1450/60, woodcut, Staatliche Graphische Sammlung, Munich.

Healing Mary

WHEN MARY APPEARS ON EARTH, miraculous cures often follow. The source of the healing is usually water, a symbol of renewal and purity. The shrines that grow up around these sites are usually the most popular of those dedicated to the Virgin; often they are grimly decorated with crutches and other mementoes that pilgrims have left behind. Such a place is Banneux, Belgium, where Mary led a young visionary to a spring with healing powers in 1933. At Lourdes, France, in 1858, Bernadette Soubirous uncovered a spring in the grotto where she had her visions of Mary, and soon the hopelessly sick were flocking there to be made well. Marpingen, Germany, where three young girls experienced apparitions of the Virgin in 1876, was the scene of so many cures that it soon became known as the German Lourdes.

On other occasions, Mary heals directly. In 1876, the Virgin brought the dying Estelle Faguette back to health for a special purpose: to encourage devotion to the Scapular of the Sacred Heart.

Miraculous cures are considered important signs that Mary, seen only by a single person or at most a few, has actually appeared and that the place where the apparition occurred is infused with her beneficent power. In this sense the recoveries are regarded as proof from the Virgin of her presence, a source of marvel to the devout and wonder to the skeptical.

Jacopo Pontormo (1494–1556), The Visitation, *San Michele, Carmignano.*

A Lady in White
Lourdes, France, 1858

*S*he has the appearance of a young girl of sixteen or seventeen. She is dressed in a white robe, girdled at the waist with a blue ribbon which flows down all around it. A yoke closes it in graceful pleats at the base of the neck; the sleeves are long and tight-fitting. She wears upon her head a veil which is also white; this veil gives just a glimpse of her hair and then falls down at the back below her waist. Her feet are bare but covered by the last folds of her robe except at the point where a yellow rose shines upon each of them. She holds on her right arm a rosary of white beads with a chain of gold shining like the two roses on her feet.

So Bernadette Soubirous described the apparition that she first saw, on February 11, 1858, in a grotto near her home in Lourdes in the French Pyrenees. Bernadette, sickly and barely literate, was then fourteen years old, the oldest child in a large, impoverished family. Not long before Bernadette's apparitions began, the Soubirous family had moved into the ground floor of an abandoned dungeon, or cachot, that a contemporary report called a "foul, somber hovel."

February 11 was a Thursday. That afternoon, Bernadette, her sister Marie, and a friend set off for a nearby river, the Gave de Pau, to gather firewood. When they reached a crossing place on a shallow side channel of the river, Marie and the friend took off their shoes and stockings and waded across. Bernadette, warned by her mother that the cold water might cause an asthma attack, stayed alone, on dry land. It was then that she heard "a great noise like the sound of a storm" and turned toward a grotto known as Massabielle on the other side of the stream. There, at the entrance, she saw a rosebush moving "as if it were windy." But the day was calm and the air still. Then, in Bernadette's own words:

*A*lmost at the same time there came out of the interior of the grotto a golden-colored cloud, and soon after a Lady, young and beautiful, exceedingly beautiful, the like of whom I had never seen, came and placed herself at the entrance of the opening above the rosebush. She looked at me immediately, smiled at me and signed to me to advance, as if she had been my mother. All fear had left me but I seemed to know no longer where I was. I rubbed my eyes, I shut them, I opened them; but the Lady was still there continuing to smile at me and making me understand that I was not mistaken.

Bernadette fell to her knees and took her rosary in her hands, but when she tried to pray, she found that her arm was paralyzed, "and it was only after the Lady had signed herself that I could do the same." When Bernadette finished reciting the rosary, "the Lady returned to the interior of the rock and the golden cloud disappeared." Bernadette then took off her shoes and stockings and waded across the icy stream toward the grotto; the water, to her surprise, felt warm on her bare feet and legs.

When they returned to Massabielle, Bernadette's companions found her on her knees and they began to tease her. On the way home, Bernadette said nothing about the white lady, but later she told her sister and swore her to secrecy. Marie could not keep the secret, however; she told their parents that evening and later told many of her friends.

Bernadette had no idea whom she had seen; in her early accounts of the visions she referred to the figure as *acqueró,* which means "that lady" or "it" or "that thing" in the Bigourdine dialect she spoke. Bernadette's mother insisted the vision was an illusion or a dream and forbade her daughter to return to the grotto. Later she relented, so, after attending Mass on Sun-

day, February 14, Bernadette, accompanied by her sister and a number of village children, returned to the grotto. They carried a vial of holy water as protection in case the figure turned out to be a demon.

At the grotto, Bernadette kneeled to pray, then called to her companions, "There she is!" (The apparition was so real to Bernadette that she was astonished that no one else could see or hear the Lady.) One child urged her to throw the holy water at the apparition, but instead Bernadette calmly poured it out on the ground, then withdrew into a trance-like state, her eyes fixed on one spot. When a rock, thrown as a prank, tumbled down from the top of the hill, the young onlookers panicked and ran. Soon the entire town knew of the apparitions.

The next six months were hectic in Lourdes, as the attention of all of France was drawn to the mysterious happenings in the obscure village in the High Pyrenees. However, most of Bernadette's eighteen visions, the highlights of which follow, occurred within six weeks.

FEBRUARY 18 (THURSDAY): When the figure appeared, Bernadette asked her to write down her words with the pen and paper that two older women, who accompanied Bernadette,

brought to the grotto. In response, the vision spoke for the first time, saying that it was not necessary to write her words down. Then she asked Bernadette to return to the grotto fifteen times as "a favor" and told the girl, "I do not promise to make you happy in this world, but in the next." The figure spoke in the local dialect.

FEBRUARY 20 (SATURDAY): During the fifth apparition, the Lady taught Bernadette a prayer which the girl said every day for the rest of her life without revealing the text.

FEBRUARY 21 (SUNDAY): While she was in a trance at the grotto, Bernadette was examined by a local physician, Pierre-Romaine Douzous, who noted that both her breathing and her pulse were normal. When the Lady appeared, she told Bernadette to "pray for sinners." Later Bernadette was summoned to the police station, where an official, Inspector Jacomet, tried unsuccessfully to intimidate her into changing her story and to make her promise not to return to the grotto.

FEBRUARY 23 (TUESDAY): In the course of the seventh apparition, *acqueró* told her "three wonderful secrets," which have been the subject of much speculation but which Bernadette kept to herself.

FEBRUARY 25 (THURSDAY): During the ninth apparition,

Bernadette went to the rear of the grotto where she began to dig with her hands in the ground until she uncovered a muddy spring. When the Lady told her, "Drink from the fountain and bathe in it," she swallowed some water and smeared mud across her face. After Bernadette left, people in the crowd continued digging until the spring was flowing freely. It was not long before miraculous cures were being attributed to the water.

MARCH 1 (MONDAY): With soldiers now in Lourdes to control the crowds, some fifteen hundred people gathered at the grotto. There they watched Bernadette, in a trance, take out a rosary, then return it to her pocket and take out another one. She later explained that the first rosary, which an ailing woman had given to her, had seemed to trouble the Lady, so Bernadette replaced it with her own.

MARCH 2 (TUESDAY): In a vision before an even larger crowd, the Lady directed Bernadette to tell the local clergy to have a chapel built on the site of the apparitions and to have the people go to the grotto in procession. Later that day, Bernadette went to the Curé Peyramale. When he accused her of lying about the apparitions, she became flustered and forgot to tell him about the chapel. So she returned that evening, only to have the curé insist that she ask the Lady her name and ask her to perform a miracle by making the rosebush at the grotto bloom.

MARCH 4 (THURSDAY): On the last of the fifteen days the Lady asked Bernadette to visit the grotto, crowds of twenty thousand attended the apparition, in hopes that they would see a miracle. When nothing out of the ordinary happened, some of the people followed Bernadette home. Later she told the curé that the Lady had just smiled when she passed on his requests and had repeated her desire for a chapel.

MARCH 25 (FEAST OF THE ANNUNCIATION): Although the fortnight of apparitions was over, Bernadette went to the grotto on this important holy day. When *acqueró* appeared, the girl again asked her name. At first the apparition only smiled, but, as Bernadette repeated the question, she opened her hands "in the manner of the Miraculous Medal," raised her eyes to heaven, and replied in dialect: "Que soy era Immaculado Conceptiou" ("I am the Immaculate Conception"). When Curé Peyramale later asked Bernadette if she knew what these words meant, she said she didn't; in fact, she had to keep repeating them so she wouldn't forget them.

The March 25 apparition confirmed what most believers in the apparitions thought—that the figure in the grotto was the Blessed Virgin Mary. However, the question of whether Bernadette, either consciously or subconsciously, knew about the Immaculate Conception (the doctrine that Mary was conceived in her mother's womb without taint of original sin) continued to be debated. Pope Pius IX had declared it official doctrine only four years before, so it is possible that Bernadette might have heard the words even if she didn't understand them.

Bernadette saw the Lady twice more—on April 7 and July 17—but received no communication from her. On April 7, Dr. Douzous became convinced that the apparitions were genuine when he observed the flame from the candle she was holding cupped in her hand touching her flesh without apparently burning her.

In the meantime, the town was being overrun by devout pilgrims and curious onlookers. When the mayor of Lourdes barricaded the grotto to discourage visitors, crowds tore the barriers down. Bernadette testified twice before a commission that the local bishop set up in July to investigate the apparitions at Lourdes. In January

Jesús Guerrero Galván (1910–1973), Madonna and Child, 1946, Mary-Anne Martin/Fine Art, New York City.

1862, the bishop declared the apparitions genuine and authorized the cult of Our Lady of Lourdes. By this time, Lourdes was well on its way to becoming one of the most popular shrines in the world. Construction of the Church of the Immaculate Conception was finished in 1872. In 1884, a medical bureau was set up, which operates to this day, to investigate the many reports of miraculous cures at Lourdes.

Bernadette returned to a life of obscurity. In 1860, she went to live at the local hospice; six years later she joined the Sisters of Notre Dame in Nevers. She died, after a long and painful illness, in 1879 at the age of thirty-five. She was beatified in 1925 and declared a saint in 1933, "not because she saw visions and experienced trances," an account of her life reads, "but because of her total commitment in simplicity, integrity, and trust." ⁓

THE GERMAN LOURDES
MARPINGEN, GERMANY, 1873

ON JULY 3, 1873, THREE EIGHT-year-old girls went into the woods near their village, Marpingen, on Germany's western border, to pick berries. They were returning home in the evening when they saw a "woman in white" with a child in her arms.

The young children were immensely agitated when they arrived home to tell the story to their parents, who were mostly skeptical. Katharina Hubertus's father sent her to bed without supper. Margaretha Kunz's mother threatened, "You will go to hell and not heaven," if she persisted with her story. Only the mother of Susanna Leist, who was the first of the three to see the figure, offered any

encouragement. "Go back into the woods tomorrow," she said. "Pray, and if you see her again ask who she is; if she says she is the Immaculately Conceived, then she is the Blessed Virgin."

The next day they returned to the woods and kneeled to pray about twenty yards from where they had seen the figure. After they had said the Lord's Prayer three times, the figure appeared again to the children. When the children asked who she was, the figure replied, "I am the Immaculately Conceived." When they asked, "What should we do?" the response was, "You should pray." In the days that followed, the Virgin encouraged them to bring the sick to her. She also said that water should be brought to the

Joseph Stella
(1877–1946),
The Virgin, 1926,
Brooklyn Museum.

spot from a spring elsewhere in the woods and that a chapel should be built.

Several cures were soon reported at the site. On the evening of July 5, the children guided the hand of a thirty-eight-year-old miner suffering from severe rheumatism to the foot of the Virgin and passed on prayers for him to say. Almost immediately he felt free of pain and disease. The next evening, July 6, two young children, one afflicted with consumption and unable to eat, the other crippled and deformed, also touched the Virgin's foot and were cured. That evening five adults from the village actually saw the Virgin, and the next morning a cross reading "Here is the place" was erected at the site of the apparition.

Before long pilgrims were flocking to Marpingen, some two thousand a day at first, a number that grew to about twenty thousand in less than ten days. On July 11, the parish priest recorded "enormous enthusiasm" in his notebook: "They came the whole night from every direction, bringing their sick in carts. . . . The Blessed Virgin is immeasurably generous. I have been reading this evening about Lourdes; it strikes me as feeble compared with the mighty current that here is breaking though all barriers. . . . At half-past eleven I could still hear the rolling of the wagons on which they were bringing the sick."

Soon Marpingen was being called the German Lourdes. (In fact, for more than a year, a far greater number of pilgrims made their way to Marpingen than to Lourdes.) To discourage the crowds, civil authorities closed the woods around the apparition site, but the children's visions continued in the village—in their homes, a school, a barn, the church, and elsewhere about the town. As the apparitions progressed, the Virgin became very familiar with the children, even joining in their games.

Meanwhile, authorities were pressuring the children to deny the apparitions, and a detective from Berlin, who was disguised as a journalist, was sent to Marpingen to question them. In early November a court found the girls guilty of disturbing the peace, disorderly conduct, and profiting by deception. They were then taken to Saar-brücken where they were incarcerated for five weeks and denied all contact with their families.

There are several reasons why Marpingen never developed into a major shrine. The apparitions there were never approved by the Church; on the contrary, it actively discouraged veneration of the Virgin of Marpingen. The government was even more hostile. A contemporary account of a visit to Marpingen described how the government harassed the local priest, Jakob Neureuter, who believed in the apparitions, and how fourteen gendarmes kept visitors away from the original apparition site. Furthermore, one of the visionaries later admitted that she had lied about seeing Mary, and, although she recanted the recantation, the damage to Marpingen—and to the town's hopes of becoming a major shrine—was done. The Marpingen apparitions also lacked an element that was present at other important nineteenth-century appearances by the Virgin: an important message to mankind. The Virgin's call to the children that they "should pray" was insipid compared with the vigorous calls to piety and warnings of doom that the Virgin Mary delivered elsewhere in that era. ❧

Leonardo da Vinci (1452–1519), The Virgin and Child with St. Anne, *Musée du Louvre.*

Scapular of the Sacred Heart
Pellevoisin, France, 1876

On February 14, 1876, as Estelle Faguette, a pious, thirty-two-year-old servant, lay dying of tuberculosis of the lungs and bones in her employer's château in Pellevoisin, France, the Virgin Mary came to her in a vision and told her, "Be patient. My Son consents to be moved. You will suffer another five days in honor of the five wounds of my Son . . ."

Mary appeared to Estelle for the next four days, and after the fifth apparition ended on February 18, Estelle knew she was cured. Her priest, who had originally assumed she was hallucinating, asked her to make the sign of the cross with her right arm, which had been swollen and paralyzed. Not only could she do this easily, but further examination showed that the swelling had disappeared, her tuberculosis had vanished, and an open wound on her arm had healed.

The previous year Estelle had written a letter to the Virgin Mary, pleading with her to intervene with her Son "to restore the health of my poor body." The letter, which she had placed in a grotto dedicated to Our Lady of Lourdes on the grounds of her employer's château, showed as much con- cern for her parents, who "have only me to help them," as for herself. She also made it clear that Mary was only the intermediary, that her cure would come from Jesus. "Please listen to my entreaties and put them before your divine Son."

In her first four visions, a blank marble votive tablet appeared between Estelle and Mary. In the fifth apparition, the tablet was decorated with a golden heart surrounded by a wreath of roses. A sword pierced the heart and underneath was inscribed: "I invoked Mary from the depth of my misery. From her Son, she obtained my complete cure. Estelle F." On this fifth visit, the Virgin complained about "the things which afflict me most . . . : the lack of respect for my Son in the Holy Communion, and the prayerful attitude people assume when their minds are really occupied with other things." She also warned Estelle: "There are snares ahead of you. People will consider you a visionary, a fanatic, a lunatic. Pay no attention. Be faithful to me. I will help you." It was the last vision Estelle would have until summer.

On July 1, 2, and 3, she had three more visions, all in the same bedroom, during which the Virgin said that she had come for "the conversion of sinners." During the July 2 apparition, the Virgin appeared framed by an oval of white, red, and yellow roses; showers of light sparkled from her hands.

By now Estelle, fully recovered, had resumed her work as a servant and no longer slept in the room where Mary had appeared. But she still visited the room whenever she could, and on some of these visits Mary appeared to her six more times between September 9 and December 8. On the first of these, Mary turned over a patch of cloth that she wore on her gown to reveal a scarlet heart emitting flames and surrounded by thorns and a cross. Blood and water came from a wound. "I love this devotion," the Virgin said. "It is here that I shall be honored."

During the eleventh apparition on September 15, Mary lamented the sad state of affairs in France: "What have I not done for France! The warning she had and yet she still refuses to listen. I can no longer restrain my Son. France will suffer."

On November 11, at one of the last apparitions, Estelle showed the Virgin a scapular of the Sacred Heart that she had made. After the Virgin praised her work, she added, "Many more must be made." On December 8 she told Estelle that she would appear no more but added the comforting words, "I shall be near you but invisible." The Virgin then held up a scapular for Estelle to kiss, telling her, "Nothing will please me more than to see this livery on all my children." Finally she told Estelle, "Fear nothing. I will help you."

Pellevoisin never attained the popularity or acquired the following of the other great apparition sites of the late nineteenth century in France, although, as one commentator wrote in the 1930s, the "Scapular of the Sacred Heart has spread across the world." And the miraculous aspects of Estelle Faguette's complete cure have never been seriously questioned—or explained. After the Virgin appeared to her in 1876, she lived another fifty years. ❧

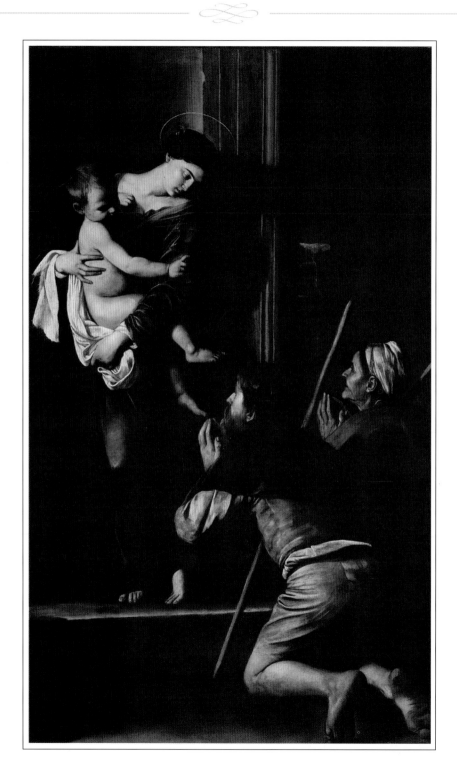

A Spring by the Road
Banneux, Belgium, 1933

Eleven-year-old Mariette Beco was helping her mother on the evening of January 15, 1933, when she pulled back a bedsheet that served as a curtain and looked out the window. She had hoped to see her younger brother who was long overdue at home. Instead, there was a lovely lady, all in white and illuminated by an unseen source of light. According to one chronicler of the event, Mariette let out a "gasp of awesome wonder and surprise" at the unexpected sight.

Mariette later provided a detailed description of the vision: a long, pleated dress of pure white material; a blue sash around her waist, its ends draped over her left knee; a transparent veil over her head, face, and shoulders; her right foot adorned with a rose of a golden hue; a gold rosary was over her right arm. When a skeptical parish priest later asked Mariette if the figure resembled a church statue of Our Lady of Lourdes, the girl replied that there was no resemblance at all. The Lady who had appeared to her in Banneux, Belgium, was much more beautiful.

When she recovered from her surprise, Mariette called out

that there was a beautiful woman in the garden, and her mother jokingly replied, "Perhaps it is the Virgin Mary." But when she looked out the window herself, she could make out only a white form that had none of the detail that Mariette was able to see. Declaring the figure to be a witch, the mother drew the curtain, but Mariette opened it again, saying, "No, it is really the Blessed Virgin. She smiles at me; she is so beautiful." But when the Lady beckoned Mariette outside, her fearful mother wouldn't let her out of the house.

The next day Mariette told the story of the vision to the parish priest, who suggested that she had been affected by reports of visions at Beauraing, Belgium, which had ended only twelve days before. In the priest's eyes, Mariette was probably an unlikely visionary. The poorly educated girl was neither pious nor religious. The year before she had stopped attending catechism classes prior to her First Communion because she found them too difficult. And, like her father, a poor farmer with a large family, she no longer went to Mass.

The vision did not recur for the next two nights. Then, on

Caravaggio (1571–1610), Madonna of the Pilgrims, *San Agostino, Rome.*

Wednesday, January 18, at seven in the evening, Mariette was praying outside her front door, when the Lady floated in over some pine trees and hovered on a white cloud a foot off the ground. When, at the Lady's signal, Mariette began to follow her, her father called her back. Mariette responded, "She calls me," and continued down the road.

Mariette went only 325 feet, but she stopped and fell to her knees three times on the way. At the third stop, those who were following her saw her place her hands in a ditch and uncover a spring. Mariette, who later explained that she was repeating the Lady's words, said: "This stream is reserved for me." Then the Lady disappeared; the apparition had lasted thirty-five minutes.

Mariette would experience six more apparitions. The next night, Thursday, January 19, the Lady identified herself as "The Virgin of the Poor" and led Mariette back to the spring, where she said, "This spring is reserved for all nations—to relieve the sick." (When Mariette reported these words, she was uncertain what they meant, not being familiar with the meaning of "nation" or "relieve.")

On Friday they returned to the spring, and the Virgin told Mariette that she would like a small chapel built on the spot. And, before she disappeared, she placed her hands on Mariette and blessed her by making the sign of the cross with her right hand. At this point, Mariette fainted.

Mariette continued her nightly vigils but there were no more apparitions for three weeks. Then, on Saturday, February 11, the Lady reappeared and again led Mariette to the spring, saying, "I am come to relieve suffering." After this apparition ended, Mariette, at her request, received Holy Communion for the first time. In Banneux this in itself was considered an unusual occurrence, because Mariette, like her family, did not attend Mass and only occasionally appeared at her catechism class.

At the Lady's next appearance, on February 15, Mariette, at the prompting of the local priest, asked Mary for a sign that would prove who she was. "Believe in me," came the answer; "I will believe in you. Pray much. Au revoir." At this meeting, the Lady also told Mariette a secret, which she never revealed.

Mariette was urged again to "pray much" at the seventh apparition—on February 20. On March 2, it was pouring rain when Mariette left her house in the evening to say her rosary

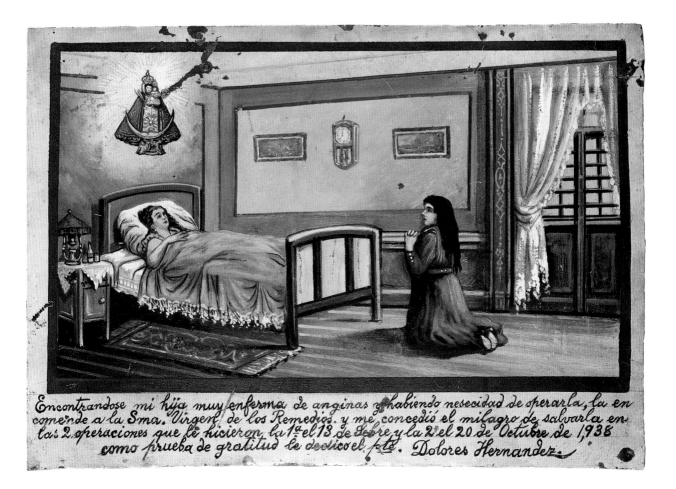

Encontrandose mi hija muy enferma de anginas y habiendo nesecidad de operarla, la encomende a la Sma. Virgen de los Remedios y me concedió el milagro de salvarla en las 2 operaciones que le hicieron la 1ª el 13 de febre y la 2ª el 20 de Octubre de 1938 como prueba de gratitud le dedico el pte. Dolores Hernandez.

Mexican,
20th century,
Ex-Voto of Dolores
Hernandez, 1938,
private collection.

while waiting for the Virgin. Then the sky cleared, and the Virgin appeared and said to Mariette, "I am the Mother of the Savior, Mother of God. Pray much." Then she again blessed the child and departed, gliding over the tops of the pine trees, with the words, "Adieu—till we meet in God." Then Mariette lost consciousness and had to be carried into her house.

The apparition of March 2, 1933, was the eighth and last appearance of the Blessed Virgin Mary at Banneux, Belgium. The first of many miraculous cures attributed to the waters of the spring that Mariette uncovered occurred less than three months later, and Banneux in time would become one of the great curative shrines of Europe. The visions of the Virgin to Mariette Beco were thoroughly investigated and, in 1949, the Bishop of Liège decreed that "the reality of the eight apparitions can and should be unreservedly acknowledged." ❧

Silent Mary

OF ALL THE APPARITIONS of the Virgin Mary, the simplest, the most tranquil, and the least controversial are those in which she appears without speaking. And because these silent appearances are made to numbers of people, they are more believable. (When an individual or only a few people see Mary, the possibility that the seers are either deluded or lying invariably arises.) And when Mary speaks, the content of her words—what she did or did not mean—becomes a source of controversy. So, in many respects, silence is more persuasive.

In Zeitoun, Egypt, where Mary appeared regularly atop a Coptic church from 1968 to 1971, hundreds reported that they witnessed the apparition. In Knock, Ireland, fourteen people saw the tableau of which Mary was the central figure. Although only four people saw Mary in a procession through the outskirts of Jaén, Spain, in 1430, they saw her from three different places, so there was little likelihood they were making up the story.

At other times, there is no need for the Virgin to speak; the seers seem to know without being told what the message is. When Mary appeared to St. Egwin in 708 and to Princess Ermesinde in 1214, they understood at once that she wanted a church to be built on the site. In both cases they had the means to make this happen.

Mexican, 19th century, Madonna on a Crescent Moon, *featherwork, Staatliche Museen zu Berlin.*

MIRACLES ON THE AVON
EVESHAM, ENGLAND, 708

WHEN HE WAS SERVING AS THE Bishop of Worcester, the eighth-century English saint named Egwin came under attack by enemies who denounced him to the king and the Archbishop of Canterbury and forced him to withdraw from his diocese. To clear his name and state his case before the Pope, Egwin journeyed to Rome. But before he left, he locked his feet into iron fetters and threw the key into the Avon River. On his arrival in Rome, while he was praying, his attendants caught a fish in the Tiber River, and when they cut it open, there was the key to Egwin's fetters. The miracle was considered proof of Egwin's piety, and soon thereafter the Pope dismissed the accusations against him and reinstated him as bishop.

On Egwin's return to England, King Ethelred gave him the stretch of land along the Avon where he had thrown the key. One day in the year 708, a herdsman named Eoves was grazing his swine on that land when he saw a vision of the Virgin and two companions singing psalms. The man told Egwin what he had seen and the bishop went there himself. While he was praying, he saw three virgins shining with a brilliant light. Although they did not speak, one, whom Egwin knew to be Mary, shone more resplendently than the others. In her hands she held a cross, and before she disappeared, she blessed him with it.

Egwin took the vision as a sign that God wanted a church on the ground where Mary appeared, and the church and abbey that he built became one of the important shrines of England. He renamed the place Evesham, after Eoves, the man who had first seen the Virgin. ❧

PRINCESS ERMESINDE'S VISION BY A FOUNTAIN
CLAIREFONTAINE, LUXEMBOURG, 1214

BORN IN THE YEAR 1186, THE devout Princess Ermesinde, the only daughter of Henry the Blind, Count of Namur and Luxembourg, grew into a woman of unusual spirit and charity. In 1214, while she was mourning the recent death of her husband, she retired to the Fountain of St. Bernard in Clairefontaine, Luxembourg (now part of Belgium), which the ascetic monk had

Vittore Carpaccio (c. 1460/5–1523/6), Virgin Reading, c. 1505, National Gallery of Art, Washington, D.C.

blessed while passing through more than sixty years before.

When she was sitting by the fountain in the shade of a tufted oak tree, Ermesinde saw a woman of incomparable beauty come down from the sky on a billowy white cloud. In her arms she carried a child who was so beautiful that Ermesinde felt it had no equal on earth. As the Lady drew near, a flock of pure white lambs with black crosses on their backs appeared and gathered around her. "Ravished with the charm of so beautiful a spectacle, Ermesinde feasted her eyes thereon, and would willingly have contemplated it forever," an account of the miracle goes. "But the vision lasted only for a moment."

When the apparition ended, the countess vowed to build and endow a convent near the fountain. Named the Religious of Our Lady of Clairefontaine, the order grew rapidly and provided care and sustenance for the poor of the surrounding countryside. Its history came to a violent end when the convent and church were sacked during the French Revolution. When the Jesuit Fathers undertook a restoration of the convent in 1894, a century after it was destroyed, they found, unharmed under the debris of the ruins, both Ermesinde's tomb and a statue of Mary that she had placed in the convent in memory of the Virgin's appearance to her.

This statue of the Virgin Mary has performed a few miracles of its own over the centuries. When Ermesinde's granddaughter, a saintly woman, would greet it, the statue would clearly nod its head in return. In more recent times, a pious servant girl in the convent regularly greeted the statue with the words "Praised be Jesus Christ," and the statue would reply, "Amen." One day, when the servant omitted the greeting, the statue of Mary rebuked her by saying, "Praised be Jesus Christ," as the girl passed by. ✥

A PROCESSION ALL IN WHITE
JAÉN, SPAIN, 1430

Master Francke (active c. 1405– after 1424), Nativity (from the Englandfahrer Altarpiece), Kunsthalle, Hamburg.

JUAN GÓMEZ WAS AWAKENED from sleep by the sound of dogs barking and a bright light outside the room which he shared with three other men. He got out of bed and put his head outside the door. There he saw a procession of five young men, all in white, carrying white crosses. Next came a lady also in white from whom, according to his testimony, "issued so

much brightness that she shone as the sun shines at its zenith on a clear day." Juan believed the hour was about midnight—on June 10, 1430. The place was the city of Jaén in northern Andalusia, Spain.

The Lady, who was half a cubit (or forearm's length) taller than the others, walked alone, trailing a train behind her and carrying an infant on her right arm. Next came a procession of twenty priests in white robes, walking in two lines on each side of the street. They were followed by a phalanx of about one hundred armed men, also in white. The sight of the men, who appeared to be carrying lances, frightened Juan. He closed the door and woke up Pedro Sánchez and told him what he had just seen and that the procession appeared to be heading toward the church of San Ildefonso.

When Pedro looked out the front door, he saw the same procession, although in his account there were more people and crosses and other minor differences in detail. As in Juan's account, the Lady appeared to be the source of a brilliant light; she was also considerably taller than the others and carried a small baby. Pedro saw one thing that Juan did not: an altar "as high as a lance" erected against the outer back wall of the church's chapel.

Two women, María Sánchez and Juana Fernández, saw the procession as well. Both were alone in their homes; their husbands, shepherds, were away. Their descriptions differed in several respects from those of the men, but, most important, where the men said the Lady was alone, the women said she walked with two other persons. María was the only one of the four to identify the Lady as Mary, whom she recognized from an image of the Virgin, a statue in the church. One of the two others with Mary, she said, was St. Ildefonso, the seventh-century Bishop of Toledo after whom the church in Jaén was named.

This saint had also experienced a famous vision of the Virgin. In 657, after he had written a book denouncing heretics who denied the virginity of Mary, she appeared to him, holding a copy of his book and surrounded by a choir of virgins. To thank him for his defense of her honor, she gave him a chasuble, saying, "Hasten, loyal servant of God, to receive from my hand a gift I have brought you from the treasure of my Son." The vestment and the stone on which Mary stood are still venerated in the cathedral at Toledo.

Jean Fouquet (c. 1420–1481), Mary and Jesus Surrounded by Seraphim and Cherubim (right half of the Melun Diptych), c. 1450, Koninklijk Museum voor Schone Kunsten, Antwerp, Belgium.

At the time of the ghostly procession through Jaén, the town was still subject to raids by Moors, who had not yet been expelled from Spain. People living outside the walls, as the four visionaries did, were particularly vulnerable. Pedro, for example, testified that at first he found the sight of the procession reassuring; the presence of all these people outside the walls of the city must mean that there was no immediate threat of attack, he assumed. But when he saw the armed men at the end of the line, his anxiety returned. Not many shared his concerns, however. Most of the people of Jaén, at least those who believed in the apparition, took it as a sign that the Virgin Mary would protect them from the Moors. ❧

A HOLY TABLEAU IN IRELAND
KNOCK, IRELAND, 1879

ACCORDING TO LOCAL LEGEND, ST. Patrick, during a stopover in Knock, Ireland, in the fifth century, declared that the village would one day be a holy place, but it certainly didn't occur to the first three people who saw the apparition on Thursday, August 21, 1879, that anything miraculous was going on. Mary McLoughlin, housekeeper to the local priest, thought that the three figures outside the church were holy statues that her employer had purchased. The second viewer, a passerby, came to the same conclusion and assumed that the parishioners would be asked to pay for them: "Another collection. God help us!" The third person noticed "something luminous" by the south gable, but rain discouraged her from looking further.

When Mary McLoughlin passed by the church again that evening, she was accompanied by Mary Beirne, the sixteen-year-old daughter of a friend, and it was she who realized that the figures were not statues and that they seemed to be floating in air.

Mary Beirne recognized two of them as the Blessed Virgin Mary and St. Joseph. She assumed the third figure was St. John the Evangelist because it resembled a statue of the saint that she had seen recently in a neighboring town. In her words, "the Blessed Virgin was life-sized, others apparently either not so big or not so high as her figure; they stood a little distance out from the gable wall, and, as well as I could judge, a foot and a half or two feet from

Geertgen tot Sint Jans (1455/65–1485/95), Night Nativity *(detail), The National Gallery, London.*

the ground." To one side and slightly behind the figures there was an altar with a cross and a lamb on it.

After the two women stared at the apparition for a few moments, Mary Beirne hurried to her home to fetch her family. She and her brother Dominick alerted others in the village and soon fourteen people were gathered at the church. From a distance of about half a mile, a fifteenth person, farmer Patrick Walsh, aged sixty-five, saw "a large globe of golden light" at about nine o'clock, but he didn't learn about the apparition until he went to town the next day.

The apparition, which was silent the entire time, lasted from about eight to nine-thirty. In some accounts the statues moved, and two young boys saw angels floating about, but, generally the seers, most of them adults, agreed on what they saw. Everyone in the group could identify the central figure as the Blessed Virgin Mary and the one on her right as St. Joseph. They took Mary Beirne's word that the third individual was St. John the Evangelist, and she, as she later testified, only "thought so, [because] at one time I saw a statue . . . very much resembling the figure which stood now before me."

The Virgin, Mary Beirne said later, "wore a large cloak of a white color, hanging in full folds and somewhat loosely around her shoulders, and fastened to the neck; she wore a crown on the head—rather a large crown— and it appeared to me somewhat yellower than the dress or robes." A particularly detailed account of the apparition, including a description of the Virgin's eye and a dark line that outlined each figure and made it stand out from the enveloping white cloud, came from thirteen-year-old Patrick Hill. When Patrick boldly approached the apparition, the figures moved back and away from him.

Another witness, Bridget French, seventy-five, dropped to her knees and exclaimed: "A hundred thousand thanks to God and to the glorious Virgin that has given us this manifestation." But when she tried to kiss the Virgin's feet, "I felt nothing . . . and wondered why I could not feel with my hands the figures which I had so plainly and distinctly seen." She also noticed that, despite the heavy rain, the ground under and around the apparition was completely dry.

The inquiries that followed the Knock apparition included attempts by experts to re-create the apparition with magic lanterns to prove that the seers had been tricked; these efforts were unsuccessful. Soon after

French, beginning of 15th century, School of Dijon, Virgin and Child *(detail), Musée du Louvre.*

August 21, miraculous cures were reported, usually by people who crumbled and ingested some of the concrete from the church wall, and Knock became a popular destination for pilgrims. Over the years, the seers were questioned many times on what they saw. In 1936, Mary Beirne told a commission reviewing events of August 21, 1879, "I am quite clear about everything I have said, and I make this statement knowing I am going before my God." She died the next year. ❧

MARY ON A CHURCH-TOP ZEITOUN, EGYPT, 1968–1971

CLOSE TO MIDNIGHT ON APRIL 2, 1968, two workers were leaving a garage across from the Coptic Church of the Holy Virgin in Zeitoun, Egypt, a district some fifteen miles north of Cairo, when one of them, a Moslem, saw a figure dressed in white on top of the church's dome. (The Copts are a Christian minority who never converted to Islam after the Moslems conquered Egypt in the seventh century.)

As the worker related: "I thought she was going to commit suicide and shouted to her to be careful. My friend called the police and I woke up the doorkeeper. He comes out and looks and cries 'It is the Virgin,' and runs to call the priest."

As news of the apparition spread, crowds began to gather at the church, where the appearances of the Virgin, which were seen by many, Moslem and Christian alike, continued throughout the following days.

The local police chief tried to persuade the gathering that the apparitions were nothing but the reflection of the streetlights, but when he ordered the electricity turned off, a Coptic woman reported, "The light of the dome remained and the vision of the Virgin became even clearer." A chemistry student at the University of Cairo also described what she saw: "She was like a statue, hands folded in front, head veiled and bent. She rose up in the sky completely and was illuminated. I first saw the halo, then I saw the Virgin completely. She came down between the palm tree and the dome . . ."

The ongoing apparitions in Zeitoun soon came under investigation by a committee appointed by the Coptic Patriarchate of Egypt and All Africa, which reported in early May: "The extraordinary visions of the past weeks have been attested to by thousands of people from all walks of life, Egyptians and foreigners of various nationalities, and groups of them had agreed on time and place of the apparition. With the facts collected, we have concluded that the apparitions are not false individual visions or mass hallucinations, but are real." The report added that many people became "true Christian believers" after seeing the visions, and that a number of miraculous cures had been reported at the church.

On May 20 in Shubra, another suburb of Cairo, a rumor of an apparition caused a stampede in which fifteen people were killed. To prevent such incidents, the police cordoned off the area around the church in Zeitoun and began charging admission—one price for entrance to the area, more to get into the church. Despite these restrictions, the crowds continued to grow and the scene soon resembled a religious festival with vendors selling incense, photographs of the apparitions, and images of the Virgin. The people were mostly urban and middle class, although there were always numbers of peasants in the crowd.

Even skeptical observers reported seeing, if not the Virgin herself, strange happenings at the church in Zeitoun. Relating her visit to Zeitoun on the evening of June 1, Cynthia Nelson, a teacher at the American University at Cairo, described "intermittent flashes of light" that caused the crowd to clap and shout, "There she is!"

Nelson's field notes on her visit continue: "Priests led the group in prayer, hymns, and made announcements over the public address system about the most recent miracles. People sat quietly in their chairs talking, eating sandwiches and drinking cold soda pop. One woman sitting next to me told me that she had been at Zeitoun for the past three days and nights, but tonight (the anniversary of the Holy Family's flight to Egypt in the first century) was the first time she had seen anything. She kept praying to the Virgin and thanking Her for coming to Egypt. She kept referring to the Virgin as *Umm-i-nur* (Mother of Light) or *Ya Habibi* (an affectionate phrase meaning O my dearest one and used by both Copts and Moslems in addressing God)."

Although the Copts, by some estimates, constitute only ten percent of the population of Egypt, the Virgin Mary is a figure familiar to both Christians and Moslems. When the Holy Family fled to Egypt to escape persecution by Herod, the Virgin is supposed to have rested for several days under a large sycamore tree that still stands only a few miles from Zeitoun, and today members of both religions consider the place holy. Moslems also believe that Mary is divine; a passage of the Koran is addressed to her: "Allah has chosen you. He has made you pure and exalted you above all women."

Between the spring of 1968 and May 1971, scores of apparitions were reported at Zeitoun. Mary's appearances were always accompanied by flights of white doves and the smell of incense. At different times, Mary has appeared carrying the Christ Child and holding out an olive branch. She has been seen as a full figure enveloped in a blue light and at other times as a bust lighted by a golden halo. In none of her many appearances has she spoken.

Mary's silence has allowed others to interpret her appearances as they will: the Coptic faithful hoped that they promised the conversion of Egyptian Moslems to Christianity; others saw in them a sign that Egypt, crushed and demoralized by its defeat in the Six-Day War against Israel the year before the apparitions began, would be renewed and reinvigorated by the presence of a figure so universally revered. ❧

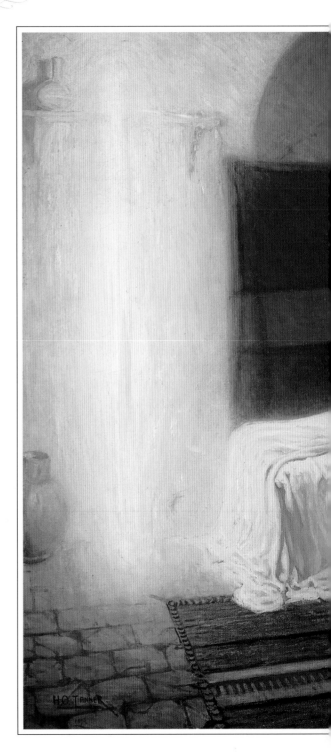

Henry Ossawa Tanner (1859–1937), The Annunciation, 1898, Philadelphia Museum of Art.

Mary of Saints

VISION OF MARY often plays an important part in the complex process by which a pious individual becomes a saint. In the case of St. Ignatius de Loyola, it was an apparition that turned him from a life of worldly pleasures to an existence wholly devoted to serving the Virgin. In thirteenth-century Florence, the Seven Servites, the only saints ever canonized as a group, were all men of the world when Mary appeared to them separately, telling them to "retire together into solitude." Similarly, a vision of Mary not only converted the French atheist Alphonse Ratisbonne to Catholicism but inspired him to lead a life that became celebrated for its piety, although he was never canonized.

St. Teresa of Avila had been well known for her spiritual powers for twenty-five years before she saw the Virgin Mary for the first time and learned that her dream of founding a convent would be fulfilled. In the fourteenth century, while still a child, St. Bridget of Sweden saw the Virgin, but it wasn't until her husband died that she founded the Brigettine Order and devoted her life to religion. In Spain, St. Alphonsus Rodríguez had several encounters with Mary in a life noted for quiet service to God. Russia's St. Seraphim of Sarov, after first seeing Mary, lived in isolation until she told him in another vision to assume direction of a convent.

Piero di Cosimo (c. 1462–1521?), The Immaculate Conception and Six Saints, *Uffizi Gallery.*

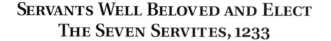

SERVANTS WELL BELOVED AND ELECT
THE SEVEN SERVITES, 1233

ON AUGUST 15, 1233, SEVEN PIOUS young men from important noble and mercantile families in Florence had simultaneous but separate visions of Mary, who appeared to them, surrounded by angels, out of a light of unnatural brightness. To each man, she said: "Leave the world, retire together into solitude, that you may fight against yourselves, and live wholly for God. You will thus experience heavenly consolations. My protection and assistance will never fail you."

The men, who were between twenty-seven and thirty-four years old, were all members of a society dedicated to the Blessed Virgin. Four of them were married. Two were already widowers, and one of the bachelors had taken a vow of celibacy. After they had shared their visions and indicated their willingness to "leave the world," they named the oldest, Bonfilius Monaldi, their leader and moved to a house outside the city walls. When they entered the city one day, a five-month-old child saw the group and uttered his first words: "Mother, those are Mary's Servants, give them an alms." The child was Philip Benizi, a future general of the order and a saint, canonized in 1671.

Soon afterward, the brethren built a monastery on a mountaintop, Monte Senario, ten miles north of Florence, a location that had been revealed to them in a vision. During Lent in 1239, they discovered that a vine they were cultivating was bearing grapes out of season, and that, according to one account, "all around smiled the verdure of spring . . ." The phenomenon was interpreted as a sign that they should form a religious order, the vines representing the seven men and the grapes those who would join their order.

On Good Friday in 1240, this purpose was confirmed when the Virgin, holding a religious habit of black cloth, appeared to them and said to her "servants well beloved and elect . . . 'I come to accomplish your desires and grant your prayers; here are the habits in which I wish you should in future be clothed; their black hue should always bring to mind the cruel dolors which I felt by reason of the Crucifixion and Death of my only Son; the Rule of St. Augustine, which I give you as the form of your religious life, will gain for you the palm prepared in heaven, if you serve me faithfully on earth.'"

Ethiopian (Gondar),
after 1730,
Our Lady Mary
at Dabra Metmaq,
wood panels,
Institute of
Ethiopian Studies,
Addis Ababa.

The Servite Order, officially the Order of the Servants of Mary, was approved in 1249 by Pope Innocent IV after his emissary, who was charged with investigating the society, had a vision of the Virgin dressed in a black mantle and of seven lilies of unusual whiteness. He took the vision to be a sign of God's favor.

In 1255, Bonfilius retired as head of the order and was replaced by Father Bonagiunta, who had come from a rich and noble family. He had once escaped death in a miraculous way: no sooner had he made the sign of the cross over poi-soned bread and wine that an enemy had sent him, than the wine flask shattered into pieces and the bread became full of worms. Father Bonagiunta died in 1257 immediately upon saying, while celebrating Mass, the words: "Into Thy hands, O Lord, I commend my spirit."

The last of the Seven Servants of Mary to die, in 1310, was Alexis, a lay brother and the only one of the seven not ordained a priest. The Seven Servites were canonized as a group, the Seven Holy Founders, in 1888. Their feast day is February 17. The Order of the Servants of Mary, or Servites, that they founded was named the fifth mendicant order during the reign of Pope Martin V (1417–31). Cloistered nuns, calling themselves the Servite Hermitesses, became affiliated with the order in 1619. The order continues in Europe and America to this day. ❧

CROWNED BY THE VIRGIN MARY
ST. BRIDGET OF SWEDEN, 1303–1373

WHEN ST. BRIDGET WAS STILL A child, she awoke suddenly one night to behold the Virgin Mary sitting on an altar near the bed. Mary, who held a crown in her hand, beckoned the child to her. "Should you like to have this crown?" she asked, and then placed it on the child's head. Three years later, when she was ten, Bridget had a vision of Christ, who appeared to her as he looked at the Crucifixion. When Bridget asked, "Lord, who has treated thee thus?" Christ replied, "Those who despise Me and who are insensible to the love I bear them."

Bridget came from a noble and pious family in Sweden. When a nun dared to criticize her mother's worldly ways, the Virgin Mary admonished the nun in a vision and foretold Bridget's birth: "I shall bless her with a daughter who, through love for me, will obtain such graces that she will be the admiration of the whole world." And at the very hour of Bridget's birth, a priest saw an angel sitting on a cloud over the house. The angel informed the priest that the family "had just been presented with a daughter whose renown will be worldwide."

Bridget married when she was fourteen and had eight children, one of whom became St. Catherine of Sweden. After her husband died, Bridget founded a monastery at Vadstena in 1346 and three years later went to Rome to obtain approval for her order. She never returned to Sweden. Her visions continued and, on a pilgrimage to the Holy Land, she saw a vision of Mary giving birth to Christ, "from whom such ineffable light and splendor radiated that the sun could not be compared to it."

Later Mary told St. Bridget: "My daughter, know that I bore my Son as you have seen, praying alone on my knees in the stable. . . . I felt no pain or difficulty when He left my body." She also saw Jesus speaking to his mother, saying: "Mother, when thou were on earth there was nothing thou did refuse to do for love of

Me; now that I am in heaven, it is just that I refuse nothing which thou do ask of Me."

In her *Revelations,* St. Bridget recorded "three remedies against thy temptations" that Mary had passed on to her:

*W*hen thou art assailed by thoughts contrary to holy purity, say, "Jesus, Son of God, who knowest all things, help me to take no pleasure in vain and sinful thoughts."

When the temptation to talk comes to thee, say, "Jesus, Son of God, who were silent before the unjust Judge, restrain my tongue till I have considered what and how to speak."

When inclined to work, or rest, or take refreshment according to thy fancy, say, "Jesus, Son of God, who were bound with cords, guide my hands and all my limbs, so that my works may all be done according to Thy good pleasure."

Many miracles were attributed to St. Bridget, who died at age seventy in 1373. When a sick woman came to her door crying for milk, Bridget, who had none, reasoned, "He who changed water into wine at Cana can also change water into milk." When she gave the woman a jug of water, the woman declared it the best milk she had ever tasted. ❧

SOLDIER INTO SAINT
IGNATIUS DE LOYOLA, 1521

WHEN THE GALLANT SPANISH nobleman Iñigo López de Loyola was young, he showed little inclination to sanctity. Although he was "ever loyal to the Faith," his secretary wrote, "he did not live in conformity with it, nor did he preserve himself from sin." High on the list of his transgressions were gambling, dueling, and "affairs with women."

In the summer of 1521, Iñigo was badly wounded in the leg while helping to defend the fort at Pamplona against French invaders. On June 29, the eve of the Day of Saints Peter and Paul, he was given the last rites;

that night St. Peter appeared to him in a vision, and he began his recovery soon afterward at his family's castle at Loyola in northern Spain.

To pass the time while he was recuperating, the soldier asked for some books. He would have preferred romances depicting the adventures of knights errant; instead he was given *The Life of Christ* by Ludolf of Saxony and *The Lives of the Saints.* Iñigo read them again and again. He was particularly impressed by the fact that St. Francis had had a spiritual conversion as the result of an illness. Eventually

PASTOR · ꝺ͛NIO · ALMIO · POPOL · XꝓIANO
A · TE · ꝺI · SIENA · ORMAI · LACURA · RENꝺO
FA · CHI · ALLEI · VOIA · OGNI · TUO · SENSO · HUMANO

VERGINE · MAꝺRE · AꝺIO · TANA · CONSORTE
ꝺEL · TUO · CALISTO · E · ꝺ͛NIO · ATANTO · ꝺONO
ASIENA · NÕ · TORAMI · ALTRO · CHE · MORTE

CALISTVS · III · SANVS · PETRI · ꝺE SENIS · PINXIT

he asked himself, "What St. Francis did, and St. Dominic did, why cannot I do?" He resolved then to live a life of poverty and seclusion and to make a pilgrimage to Jerusalem.

Unable to sleep one night, he left his bed and kneeled before a picture of the Virgin. While he was praying, an earthquake shook the castle and Mary appeared with the Christ Child in her arms. During this apparition, she accepted his vow to dedicate his life to her. Soon afterward, and before he was fully recovered, he left home and crossed northern Spain on a mule to the sanctuary dedicated to the Virgin Mary in Montserrat.

On this trip, he encountered a Moorish gentleman, a "Mohammedan," who denied the virginity of Mary after the birth of Christ. After they parted compa-ny, it occurred to Ignatius, as he came to be called, that perhaps he should have punished the infidel for his blasphemy. But still unsure, he let his mule decide: if it followed the Moor, he would extract punishment. But the mule took another road, saving Ignatius from committing a bloody deed he would have later regretted.

Ignatius spent a year in prayer at Manresa, close to Montserrat, where he composed his famous *Spiritual Exercises*. In 1523 he made a pilgrimage to Jerusalem, then returned to Spain to begin studies in Latin and philosophy. With six followers, he founded the Society of Jesus in 1534. In 1540, the Society was approved by the Pope and Ignatius was named the Society's first general. Ignatius died in 1556 and was canonized in 1622. ⸎

"GOD PRESERVE US FROM STUPID NUNS"
ST. TERESA OF AVILA, 1561

WHEN ST. TERESA OF AVILA, founder of the order known as the Reformed Carmelites, had her first vision of Mary, she had been a nun for some twenty-five years and was well known for her visions and spiritual gifts. Devotion to religion and God were evident in her from a very early age. She was only seven when she convinced her brother to run away to Africa (a plot that was quickly foiled by their parents) in hopes that the Moors would oblige them with martyrs' deaths and a quick route to heaven. When she was thirteen, her mother died and Teresa turned to Mary. "I went in my distress to an image of Our Lady," she wrote, "and, weeping bitterly, begged her to be my mother."

Sano di Pietro (1406–1481), Madonna Appearing to Pope Callistus III, *Pinacoteca Nazionale, Siena.*

The visions she experienced were not always to her liking, and she often asked God to show her another path to enlightenment and salvation. In her raptures, Teresa was also subject to bodily levitation, and on occasion she was supposed to have asked fellow nuns to hold her on the ground so she would not cause a commotion in public. Her communications with God were frequently two-way, and Teresa, who was noted for her witty tongue, once chided Him for treating His "friends" so poorly. "That could be why You have so few of them," she suggested.

In Teresa's first vision of Mary, in 1561, the Virgin, who appeared with St. Joseph beside her, dressed Teresa in a robe "of great whiteness and clarity," then took her by the hand and told her that her hopes to found a convent to serve St. Joseph would be fulfilled. Mary also promised that she and Joseph would watch over it. "Then she seemed to hang around my neck a very beautiful gold collar from which hung a cross of great value. The gold and the stones were so different from those of this world that there is no comparing them; their beauty is quite unlike anything we can imagine here. Nor can the imagination rise to any understanding of the nature of the robe, or to any conception of its whiteness. Such

was the vision that the Lord was pleased to send to me that by comparison everything here on earth seems, as you might say, a smudge of soot."

The Virgin, "who looked to me almost like a child," and St. Joseph lingered a while, "bringing me the greatest joy and bliss—more I believe than I had ever known before, and I wished it would last for ever." They then rose into the sky accompanied by "a great multitude of angels . . ."

Although Teresa's proposal to found a convent based on austerity was opposed by both ecclesiastical and civil authorities, she was able to overcome the obstacles and opened the convent of St. Joseph in 1562 with thirteen nuns in residence. She went on to found sixteen other convents in which the nuns, who wore coarse wool habits and leather sandals, lived a life of poverty, hardship, and solitude. Teresa selected nuns for her convents based on their intelligence and good judgment. "God preserve us from stupid nuns," she once said.

St. Teresa's most famous vision, which occurred in 1559, was not of Mary. In it, she saw an angel: "In his hands I saw a great golden spear, and at the iron tip there appeared to be a point of fire. This he plunged into my heart several times. . . . The sweetness caused by this intense pain is so extreme

Francisco de Zurbarán (1598–1664), The Young Virgin, c. 1635/40, Metropolitan Museum of Art.

that one cannot possibly wish it to cease, nor is one's soul then content with anything but God." This vision was the inspiration for Bernini's famous sculpture, an extremely sensual work, at the church of Santa Maria della Vittoria in Rome.

St. Teresa died in 1582 and was canonized in 1622. ❧

A HOLY MAN ON MAJORCA
ST. ALPHONSUS RODRÍGUEZ, 1571–1617

BORN IN SPAIN IN 1531, ALPHONSUS Rodríguez devoted his life to God after his wife and child died in 1563. Soon afterward he had a vision of Mary offering his soul to God, and he joined the Jesuits as a lay brother. From 1571 to his death in 1617, he served as a hall porter in a Jesuit college on the island of Majorca. There, when he called on Mary to aid him against temptation, she appeared and said, "Alphonsus, my son, where I am you have nothing to fear."

Despite his lowly position, Rodríguez had considerable spiritual influence on others.

He once advised a monk: "Have recourse to Mary, and you may rest assured you will obtain what you ask." When his superior tested his obedience by ordering him to embark on a journey although there were no ships in port, Rodríguez said that he would walk as far as he could on water, "happy at least that I had been as obedient as was in my power."

Alphonsus Rodríguez was canonized in 1888. A poem by Gerard Manley Hopkins admiringly contrasts his quiet saintliness with the deeds of martyrs and other holy men. ❧

A HERMIT HEALED BY MARY
ST. SERAPHIM OF SAROV, 1759–1833

SAINT SERAPHIM OF SAROV WAS born in 1759 in Kursk, Russia. As a young man of nineteen, he entered a monastery at Sarov near Moscow and worked there as a carpenter. After some time he left the community to live as a hermit in the wilderness,

returning to the monastery—a two-hour walk—only on Sundays. According to legend, the meager ration he received from the monks was miraculously multiplied so that he could share it with the wild animals he lived among.

Pedro Berruguete (c. 1450–1503/4), Virgin Appearing to a Community of Dominicans, c. 1490/99, Museo del Prado.

In 1804, Seraphim was attacked by three brigands who concluded that the hermit's radiant happiness could only be caused by gold, which they assumed he had hidden in his hut. Although he was tall and strong and was carrying an ax when they attacked him, Seraphim did not resist, and the robbers beat him with the handle of his own ax until he was nearly dead. While he was in a coma in the monastery, the Virgin Mary, accompanied by the apostles Peter and John, appeared to him, and he began to recover slowly. After convalescing under the care of the monks, Seraphim, now stooped and supporting himself with a cane, returned to the woods. The robbers were so astounded by his recovery that they came to him and asked him to forgive them, which he did.

Andrea Mantegna (c. 1431–1506), Madonna with Child and Saints, *Galleria Sabauda, Turin.*

After submitting himself to an ordeal of silence, in which he spoke to no one from 1807 to 1810, Seraphim returned to the monastery. Another vision of Mary convinced him to end his isolation and devote himself to the direction of a convent, the Sisters of Diveiev, and to those seeking spiritual guidance and enlightenment. At times there were as many as two thousand people at the monastery at Sarov waiting for a chance to see him.

In March 1831, Mary, this time flanked by John the Baptist and John the Divine, appeared to him again and told him, "Soon, my friend, you will be one of us forever." Seraphim later said that the apparition, which was witnessed by a nun from the convent of Diveiev, had lasted for four hours.

Seraphim was found dead in his cell on January 14, 1833. His clothes had been burned by a candle he was holding when he died and his face was turned toward an icon of Mary. ⁓

AN ATHEIST IN ROME
ALPHONSE RATISBONNE, 1842

ALPHONSE RATISBONNE WAS BORN in 1814, the ninth son of a wealthy family of Jewish bankers from Strasbourg, France. Worldly and intellectually gifted, he received his law degree in Paris before returning home to join his uncle in the banking business. Like his family, he wrote, "I was a Jew in name; that was all. I did not even believe in God." His aversion to all things religious was aggravated when his brother Théodore, a convert, became a Jesuit priest and wrote a book on the life of St. Bernard. "I did not wish even to look at him," Alphonse wrote later.

In January 1842 he found himself by chance in Rome where he visited the great Chris-

tian churches and also "the wretched spectacle" of the Jewish ghetto, an experience that stirred in him a sense of his own ethnic identity. In Rome he met Théodore de Bussières, a fellow Frenchman, a former Protestant converted to Catholicism. De Bussières asked Ratisbonne to do two things, and Ratisbonne, in the spirit of taking a dare, agreed. The requests were that he wear a Miraculous Medal around his neck and that he recite, twice a day, a prayer written by St. Bernard:

*R*emember, O most gracious Virgin Mary, that never was it known that anyone who fled to thy protection, implored thy help, or sought thy intercession was left unaided. Inspired by this confidence, I fly unto thee, O Virgin of virgins my Mother. To thee I come: before thee I stand, sinful and sorrowful. O Mother of the Word Incarnate, despise not my petitions, but graciously hear and answer me. Amen.

Ratisbonne was supposed to leave Rome for Naples but, for reasons that even he didn't understand, he kept delaying his departure. On the night of January 19 he wrote, "I awakened with a start and saw before me a large cross of special shape without the body of Christ being attached to it," which he would later identify as the cross on the Miraculous Medal. When he arose that morning, he thought no more about it.

That day Ratisbonne accompanied de Bussières to the Church of Sant'Andrea delle Frate, where his companion left him while he attended to other business. While Ratisbonne wandered around the church, a black dog blocked his path for a moment. "Then," his narrative continues, "the church itself seemed to disappear; and I saw nothing at all. . . . Or I should rather say, O my God, that I saw one thing alone."

I raised my eyes; I could no longer see anything of the building. All the light seemed as if it were concentrated in one of the chapels, and in the midst of its shining there stood upon the altar the Virgin Mary as she is shown on the [Miraculous] medal, beautiful, glorious, and embodying at once both majesty and kindness. A force which I could not resist drew me toward her. The Virgin made a sign with her hand that I should kneel and she seemed to say: "It is well." She did not actually speak to me, but I understood as if she had.

When de Bussières found him, Ratisbonne was on his knees before a chapel dedicated to St. Michael. As he was helped up, Ratisbonne began sobbing and kissing his Miraculous Medal. Later in the presence of a priest, all he could say was, "I have seen her! I have seen her!"

On January 31, Ratisbonne was baptized and confirmed and received his first Holy Communion; among those present was his priest-brother Théodore. In June he entered the Jesuit order and later joined his brother to work for the conversion of the Jews. He died on May 6, 1884, in Jerusalem; his last words were: "All my wishes have been granted!" A canonical inquiry into his apparition and conversion stated that "it is certain that a true and notable miracle, the work of God, through the intercession of the Blessed Virgin, did produce the instantaneous and complete conversion of Alphonse Ratisbonne." ❧

Jusepe Ribera (1591?–1652), The Holy Family with Saints Anne and Catherine of Alexandria, 1648, Metropolitan Museum of Art.

Our Lady of Sorrow

WHEN MARY CRIES, it is usually taken as a sign of her sorrow—at the crucifixion of her Son or the sorry state of mankind—but there are other interpretations. By crying, some believe, she establishes a rapport with those who have led hard and discouraging lives. When the two young shepherds at La Salette first saw a weeping lady in 1846, it didn't occur to them that she was the Virgin; they just assumed that the woman had been abused by her family, as they had been by theirs.

In Castelpetroso, Italy, in 1888, a number of people saw a mournful Mary in a fissure in the rocks; they could identify her as *Mater Dolorosa* by the seven wounds on her body, symbols of her seven sorrows. In 1483, Mary appeared as a weeping young child to a peasant in El Torn, Spain; he had first heard her sobs coming from behind a locked church door. Mary's tears often flow from a painting or sculpture. In Chicago in 1986, an icon of Mary began crying in an Eastern Orthodox church founded for Albanian refugees; it was widely assumed that the tears were caused by Albania's suffering under a repressive government. But no one really knows why Mary weeps. After a statue shed tears in Sicily in 1953, Pope Pius XII posed, in a radio broadcast, a question that is still being asked: "Will men understand the mysterious language of those tears?"

El Greco (Domenikos Theotocopoulos; 1541–1614), Mater Dolorosa, *c. 1585, Thyssen-Bornemisza Collection, Lugano.*

Behind a Chapel's Locked Doors
El Torn, Spain, 1483

In 1483, a time when outbreaks of plague were causing fear and uncertainty in Spain, a peasant named Miguel Noguer, returning home from a day of hunting, stopped to pray at a chapel dedicated to the Virgin Mary. The chapel, which was no longer used, was locked, so Noguer knelt by the entrance and, according to the official record of the happening, "prayed as God ordained."

When he had finished saying his prayers, he rose to his feet and started to leave. He was stopped by the cries and sobs of a child inside the church; then the doors suddenly opened and there, three or four paces within the chapel, he saw a beautiful young girl of seven or eight, dressed all in white. She was wringing her hands and crying, asking Jesus Christ to have pity on His people. Although Noguer was dazzled by the sight and very frightened, he managed to summon up the courage to ask her, "O sweet child, will you tell me what is troubling you so."

The girl replied: "My son, I charge you by your soul to charge the soul of the men of the parishes of El Torn, Milleras, El Salent, and Sant Miguel de Campmaior to charge the souls of the priests to ask the people to pay up the tithes and all the duties of the church and restore other things that they hold covertly or openly which are not theirs to their rightful owners within thirty days. . . . And second that they should cease and desist from blaspheming and they should pay the usual *charitats* mandated by their dead ancestors."

The Virgin Mary, as she identified herself to Noguer, ordered him to tell the local bishop, "on his soul," to reopen the chapel without delay. If these orders were not carried out, and if the people did not cease their blasphemous ways, Mary told the peasant, she would send what Noguer described to his questioners as "great mortal epidemics of bubonic plague over the land." The apparition ended when the chapel doors closed just as they had opened, as if by themselves.

The apparition occurred on Thursday, November 30. Because Noguer, a property owner and farmer, was respected in his community, his word on the apparition was enough to convince the bishop to reopen the chapel, but the effect of Mary's message on religious and tithing practices has not been recorded. The plague, the threat of which was at the heart of Mary's message, continued; there were serious outbreaks in Catalonia, the region in which El Torn is located, until 1530. Noguer lived into the sixteenth century; he was buried, as he asked to be in his will, in a grave located by the door of the chapel where the apparition of the Virgin Mary took place. ❧

TEARFUL LADY ON A ROCK
LA SALETTE, FRANCE, 1846

LATE ON THE AFTERNOON OF September 19, 1846, two young herders awoke from a nap in a meadow high in the French Alps to find that the cows they were tending had wandered off. As they were rounding up the animals, fourteen-year-old Mélanie Mathieu looked into a ravine and saw a bright orb of light.

Mélanie called her companion, Maximin Giraud, aged eleven, and, as the pair watched with a mixture of fear and astonishment, the ball of light was transformed into a woman. She was seated on a rock, weeping, with her face in her hands. Then she rose, and with her arms crossed on her breast, approached, assuring the children in a soothing voice that they had nothing to fear.

Speaking in French, which the children, who spoke a local dialect, did not understand well, the weeping Lady delivered a long complaint about the neglected state of religion during that time of social and political turmoil in France. "If my people will not obey, I shall be compelled to loose my Son's arm," she warned. "It is so heavy, so pressing that I can no longer restrain it. How long I have suffered for you! If my Son is not to cast you off, I am obliged to entreat Him without ceasing. But you take no least notice of that. No matter how well you pray in the future, no matter how well you act, you will never be able to make up to me what I have endured for your sake."

When the children first saw the woman weeping, they assumed that she had been abused by her family, just as they had been mistreated. But the woman hardly had the look of a victim. On her head she wore a headdress capped by a crown that was ringed with roses. Pearls adorned both her long white dress and her slippers, which were decorated with gold buckles and roses.

In her words to the children, she went on to complain that

people no longer observed the Sabbath and that they took her Son's name in vain: "This it is which causes the weight of my Son's arm to be so crushing." (At times during this discourse, only one or the other of the children could hear her.) After telling each child a secret, she warned of a famine to come: "The grown-ups will pay for their sins by hunger. The grapes will rot and the walnuts will turn bad." But, she added, "if people are converted, the rocks will become piles of wheat, and it will be found that the potatoes have sown themselves."

The interview ended with the Lady asking the young cowherds if they prayed, and, when they admitted that they did not, she spoke of the importance of saying "at least an Our Father and a Hail Mary" morning and night. Then, in a curious exchange with Maximin, she reminded him of the time that he had seen spoiled grain with his father, an event that he had completely forgotten. Before she glided away, she twice commanded the children: "You will make this known to all my people."

After the strange vision faded, Mélanie at first suspected that the lovely Lady might be, in her words, "a great saint." It was only after they had told the story to the farmers who employed them that the mother of one of them speculated that the figure must be the Blessed Virgin Mary.

Mélanie and Maximin were questioned rigorously about what they had seen, a process that included separate interrogations, trick questions, and threats, but they remained steadfast and consistent in their story. Their supporters pointed out that they had met only two days before, and therefore would have had little opportunity to concoct such an elaborate tale. Nor did they seem particularly friendly or compatible. Mélanie's somewhat morose nature clashed with Maximin's high spirits.

Twice the cowherds were taken back to the site of the apparition to reconstruct the event. On the second trip, a man accompanying them broke off a piece of the rock where the Lady had sat and a spring burbled out of the ground beside it. Later, an ailing woman in town drank some of the water, and in nine days she was cured.

La Salette soon became a popular destination for pilgrimages—and remains one to this day. On the first anniversary of the apparition, some fifty thousand people crowded the hillside for services. In 1851, Bishop de Bruillard, with papal approval, declared that "the apparition of the Blessed Virgin to two herders

Cruz López (b. 1974), Our Lady of Sorrows/Nuestra Señora de los Dolores, 1994, santos figure, Maxwell Museum of Anthropology, Albuquerque, New Mexico.

on September 19, 1846, on the mountain of the Alpine chain situated in the parish of La Salette, . . . bears in itself all the marks of truth, and the faithful have grounds to believe it indubitable and certain." In 1879 the Cardinal Archbishop of Paris consecrated a church at La Salette and dedicated a statue of the Virgin as she appeared in 1846 as Our Lady of La Salette.

After the apparition of 1846, the two seers of La Salette led troubled lives. In the years that followed, both failed in their attempts to dedicate themselves to God— Mélanie in a convent, Maximin by studying for the priesthood. Mélanie, who died in 1904, claimed to have had other visions and revelations and eventually published a book on her experiences at La Salette that was banned by the Church. Maximin, in the course of an aimless life, at one time caused a small scandal when he endorsed a liqueur called La Salettine by allowing the distiller to use his name on the label. He died at age forty. ✧

THE WOUNDS OF SORROW
CASTELPETROSO, ITALY, 1888

IT WAS THE DAY BEFORE THE Feast of the Compassion of Our Blessed Lady, March 22, in the year 1888. Two peasant women, Fabiana Cecchino and Serafina Giovanna Valentino, had gone off into the hills near the town of Castelpetroso in southern Italy to look for lost sheep, and when they returned they were hysterical. They had seen a light coming from a fissure in the rocks, and on looking closer, they had seen the Virgin Mary, her face very pale and beautiful, her hair disheveled. They recognized her as Our Lady of Sorrows because of the seven bleeding sword wounds on her body, the traditional symbol of her seven sorrows.

Soon others were seeing apparitions at the same place on the mountainside. "The report of this event spread far and wide," the bishop of the local diocese later wrote, "and very many persons, young and old, visited the spot. Day after day hundreds of the faithful thronged to the sacred place, many of them passing the whole night there, in sighs and tears and prayers."

Most often the Virgin appeared as Our Lady of Sorrows, or *Mater Dolorosa,* but people occasionally saw her in other guises—as Our Lady of Mount Carmel or Our Lady of the Rosary. She was usually alone, but at times appeared in company with St. Michael, St. Anthony, or St. Sebastian. Some-

times there was a flock of angels with her. An elderly priest, who had derided the apparitions, later testified that, on May 16, 1888, having "felt a desire to visit the place," he looked into one of the fissures, and saw "with great clearness, Our Lady, like a statuette, with a little child in her arms. After a short interval I looked again at the same spot; and, in place of the Most Holy Virgin I saw, quite clearly, the dead Savior bearing the crown of thorns and all covered with blood."

In that same month of May a spring appeared at the place on the mountain and soon remarkable cures and miracles were being attributed to the water. In one published instance, the father of a six-year-old boy, who had been mute from birth, went to the spring and sent some of the water home to his wife. When the boy drank it, he was able to speak for the first time.

The cornerstone for a church at the place of the apparition was laid in May 1890. ✥

THE LANGUAGE OF TEARS
SYRACUSE, SICILY, 1953

ANTONINA AND ANGELO IANNUSO were married on March 21, 1953, and went to live at the groom's brother's house at Via Degli Orti 11 in Syracuse, Sicily. There they hung an ordinary,

plaster-of-Paris image of the Virgin over their bed. Antonina was soon pregnant, but her pregnancy turned out to be difficult; she had frequent convulsions which were sometimes

Peruvian, 18th century, Cuzco School, Our Lady of Sorrows/Nuestra Señora de los Dolores, *private collection, Venice.*

accompanied by temporary blindness. In the early hours of August 29, 1953, an attack left her unable to see. Then, at about eight-thirty the same morning, her vision was restored. In her own words:

I opened my eyes and stared at the image of the Madonna above the bedhead. To my great amazement I saw that the effigy was weeping. I called my sister-in-law Grazie and my aunt, Antonina Sgarlata, who came to my side, showing them the tears. At first they thought it was an hallucination due to my illness, but when I insisted, they went close up to the plaque and could well see that tears were really falling from the eyes of the Madonna, and that some tears ran down her cheeks onto the bedhead.

The image of the Madonna, depicting Mary offering her immaculate heart, burning with fire, had been mass-produced in a mold, dried in the sun, and then sealed with varnish and painted. It was then screwed to a black opaline panel. The plaque, about sixteen inches tall, had been a wedding present.

The image of Mary wept for four days. During that time it was moved repeatedly from inside to a wall outside the house, so that the crowds could see it, to an altar across the street where the rosary was recited. On the first day it was taken to the police station. It stopped weeping once it was there and did not start again until it was returned to the house. People began collecting samples of the tears on pieces of cloth and dabs of cotton, and soon miraculous cures were being reported.

On the morning of the fourth and last day, Tuesday, a commission of experts appointed by the Church detached the image of Mary from the plaque itself, and collected samples of the tears in a sterilized tube and sent it off to a lab to be analyzed. The Madonna stopped weeping at eleven-forty that morning.

It has been said that no miracle has ever been so thoroughly examined or so quickly approved by the Catholic Church. The results of the laboratory examination were released ten days later; it explained that the tears from the image had been compared with those of an adult and a child and that the liquid from the image was, without question, "analogous to human tears." In December of the same year the Archbishop of Palermo stated in a radio broadcast that "after careful sifting of the numerous reports, after having noted the positive results of the diligent chemical analysis under which the tears gathered were examined, we have unanimously announced the judgment that

the reality of the facts cannot be put in doubt."

Within a few years nearly three hundred cures were attributed to the Weeping Madonna. Antonina Iannuso, whose son was born the following Christ- mas Day, also recovered completely after seeing the Weeping Madonna. The plaque—*La Madonnina delle Lacrime*—is now enshrined above the altar in a sanctuary built especially to accommodate her. ❧

TEARS FOR ALBANIA
CHICAGO, 1986

WHEN THE VERY REVEREND Archimandrite Philip Koufos, pastor of the St. Nicholas Albanian Orthodox Church in Chicago, noticed streaks of moisture on the icon of the Blessed Virgin Mary, he was busy lighting candles in preparation for the feast day, on December 6, 1986, of the church's patron. At first he thought that two women helping him had inadvertently splashed water on the icon as they cleaned, but a closer look showed that tears were welling up in the eyes of the Virgin.

Father Koufos summoned the two parishioners, Lillian George and Bessie Tolbert. As they approached the iconostasis, or icon screen, that separates the sanctuary from the rest of the church, they too could see the tears falling from her eyes. Then, as the three watched in awe, moisture began to spurt from the image's fingers.

The icon, which typically portrays Christ as a small, wise adult on Mary's arm, was painted in 1964, three years after the church was founded to serve Chicago's Albanian community. Father Koufos, who is of Greek descent, explains that there is considerable speculation that the weeping was in response to the actions of the repressive government in Albania, where, he says, even making the sign of the cross was against the law.

The icon wept for seven months; since then it has wept twice for about a week, but "not copiously," according to Father Koufos. There have been other miraculous manifestations; during one Holy Week a small lighted cross appeared on her face. Her expression has been seen to change: she appears sad at times, smiling at others. Also, the icon never has to be dusted or cleaned, a highly unusual situation in a church where professional cleaners have to be called in to remove the smoky residue of countless candles lighting the icons that cover the walls. There have been sixty dramatic cures and many conversions attributed to the icon.

Since the icon of the Virgin Mary began weeping in 1986, more than three million people, including the Patriarch of Constantinople, have come to see it. This influx has strained the limited resources of the St. Nicholas Albanian Orthodox Church, which Father Koufos describes as "just a parish church," with fewer than three hundred families. ✄

Geertgen tot Sint Jans (1455/65–1485/95), Man of Sorrows (detail), Museum Catharijneconvent, Utrecht.

"Build Me Here a Church"

URELY NO FIGURE IN HISTORY is responsible for the construction of more churches than the Virgin Mary. In her very first earthly appearance—to St. James at Saragossa, Spain, in A.D. 40—she commanded him to erect a church, the first one ever built in her honor. And she has been requesting churches ever since. In Rome, in 325, she outlined the shape of the future Santa Maria Maggiore with an unusual midsummer snowfall; in Walsingham, England, a heavy dew marked the dimensions of the church built in 1061; in Monte Vergine, Italy, in 1119, a flock of white doves marked the place.

Mary can be persistent in her quest for churches. In Guadalupe, Mexico, she literally flew over a mountain to block the path of the peasant Juan Diego, who was trying to avoid her—and the daunting task of building the chapel she wanted. About 1104, she temporarily crippled a woman who ignored her request for a church in Thetford, England.

Nor is Mary above helping these projects along. In Le Laus, France, in 1664, a poor woman appeared from nowhere and donated a gold coin, enough to get the work on a chapel started. More recently, in 1815, Mary caused a bridge of ice to form on the St. Lawrence River so that stone for a new church could be brought across. In these various ways, Mary sees to it that monuments to her are erected.

Giovanni-Antonio Badile (1516/17–1562), Madonna and Child *(detail), Santa Maria Ala Scala, Verona.*

OUR LADY OF THE PILLAR
SARAGOSSA, SPAIN, A.D. 40

THE STORY OF OUR LADY OF THE Pillar begins with the apostle St. James "the Greater" in Spain, where he went to preach the gospel some years after the Crucifixion. Tradition holds that in A.D. 40, while James was at Saragossa and discouraged by what he perceived to be the failure of his mission, the Virgin appeared to him, transported there on a throne from Jerusalem by a band of angels. (It is possible that Mary was still alive when this miracle occurred.) After James threw himself on the ground at the sight of her, she gave him a column of jasper and a small wooden statue of herself, saying: "This place is to be my house, and this image and column shall be the title and altar of the temple that you shall build."

The chapel that James subsequently built was the first ever dedicated to the honor of the Virgin Mary. The chapel and several churches that replaced it were destroyed, but the pillar and the statue survived. Today they are housed in a church built in the seventeenth century and dedicated to the Virgin of the Pillar. The wooden statue of the Virgin Mary is a mere fifteen inches tall. It depicts her supporting the Christ Child on her left arm; he holds a small bird in his hand. After Compostella, where St. James is believed to be buried, Saragossa is the most popular Christian shrine in Spain.

After building the chapel, James returned to Jerusalem where he became the first apostle to be martyred for the faith when he was executed by King Herod Agrippa in A.D. 44. His legend continues, however, with the story of how his disciples took his remains aboard a ship that was propelled—by divine power, since it had neither rudder nor sail—to Galicia, now northwestern Spain, a territory then ruled by a pagan queen whom James, in his mission to Spain, had failed to convert. The disciples said to her: "Our Lord Jesus Christ hath sent to you the body of His disciple, so that the man you would not receive alive you shall receive dead." And they asked her to provide a burial place for the holy man.

The queen sent them to the mountains to find oxen to pull a cart bearing James's body, knowing that these oxen were really wild bulls that would attack the disciples. But when the ferocious animals charged, the disciples made the sign of the cross before them, and the bulls became calm. When the queen saw the wild beasts docilely pulling a cart, she immediately embraced Christianity.

The disciples let the bulls show the way, and after pulling the cart about ten miles, the animals stopped in a field. Here the apostle was buried in a marble sarcophagus, but the burial place was soon forgotten. Eight centuries later, a hermit who was a holy man was led there by an unusual array of stars in the sky. When St. James's remains were uncovered, King Alfonso II declared him the patron saint of all Spain and called on his spirit to inspire the king's countrymen in their struggle to expel the Moors from Spain. Alfonso had a church built over the place where the tomb of St. James was uncovered; and the city that grew up around the shrine was named Compostella, or starry field, after the heavenly display that led to its discovery. Compostella soon became the principal place of pilgrimage in Spain, and it remains so to this day with many still going there on foot. ❧

A Snowfall on a Hill
Rome, 352

Each year on August 5, in a ceremony commemorating the miraculous origins of one of Rome's most ancient Christian churches (and now one of the largest Catholic churches in the world), white flowers representing snow fall from the ceiling of a chapel in which a revered portrait of the Virgin Mary is kept. Thus Santa Maria Maggiore (St. Mary Major) annually celebrates its birth in the year 352.

The story begins with an aging Roman nobleman and his wife who, because they had no children, wished to use their wealth to honor the Virgin Mary. After they had prayed to God for guidance, Mary appeared to them both in a dream, telling them to build a church for her on the Esquiline, one of Rome's seven hills. The place, she said, would be marked by snow, a miracle indeed since Rome in August is at its hottest.

The next morning, August 5, the aristocrat went to tell Pope Liberius about his vision of Mary, only to learn that the Pope had had the same dream. They went together to the Esquiline where they found snow covering an area of ground matching the form and size of a church. Once this area was marked off, the snow disappeared.

To further honor the Virgin, the Pope selected a portrait of

Mary, nearly five feet high and painted on a thick cedar slab, which the Empress St. Helena had brought to Rome from Palestine. (Another legend holds that it was painted by St. Luke the Evangelist.) In it, Mary wears a dark blue mantle around her shoulders and holds the Christ Child on her left arm. A number of miracles have been attributed to the painting. According to the Reverend J. Spencer Northcote in his book *Celebrated Sanctuaries of the Madonna* (1868), a cholera epidemic afflicting Rome promptly ended in 1837 when Pope Gregory XVI

carried the work in a procession. In gratitude, "the Pope made an offering of two golden crowns, richly ornamented with precious stones (one for the Mother, the other for the Son) to replace the crowns of silver . . . which had been lost during some of the numerous political disturbances to which the city has been so often subjected."

The church was first called Basilica Liberiana after the Pope who consecrated it. In the next century Sixtus III rebuilt the church on a grander scale after the Council of Ephesus reaffirmed the Virgin Mary as

Bartolomé Estebán Murillo (1617–1682), The Foundation of Santa Maria Maggiore in Rome: The Patrician's Dream, c. 1662/65, Museo del Prado.

the mother of God; he renamed the church Basilica Sixti. In the middle of the seventh century, a relic from Bethlehem—the manger of the Christ Child—was brought to the church, after which it was called St. Mary of the Crib. Pope Paul V built a chapel to hold the venerable painting in 1613.

The story of the miraculous snowfall on the Esquiline might not hold up under what Rev. Northcote called "a minute examination into the evidence upon which the story rests." There are theories today that a church might have been built on the site before the 352 date. Still, Pope Benedict XIV (1740–58) reaffirmed the story when he proclaimed: "It must be acknowledged that nothing is wanting to enable us to affirm with moral certainty that the prodigy of the snow is true." ❧

"Unto Her Laud and Honor"
Walsingham, England, 1061

The miraculous history of Walsingham, England, begins in the year 1061 when a widow, a lady of the manor named Richeldis of Faverches, had three visions of Mary. In each the Virgin transported Richeldis "in spirit" to the House of the Annunciation in Nazareth where the angel Gabriel, more than a millennium before, had told Mary that she would give birth to the Son of God. The Virgin commanded Richeldis to measure the house and to build, "unto her laud and singular honor," an exact replica in Walsingham, so that "all who sought her there might find succor." The replica of her house would also serve to remind the devout of the good news carried to the house by the angel Gabriel.

While the widow was pondering exactly where to build the house in Walsingham, a heavy frost completely covered the ground except for two bare spots, each the exact dimensions of the holy house. Richeldis chose one that was located near a pair of twin wells, but after the workmen had laid a foundation, they were inexplicably unable to attach the house to it. Richeldis spent one night in prayer over the problem and the next morning discovered that the foundation had been miraculously transported to the other site some two hundred feet away.

According to contemporary observers, the Holy House at Walsingham was constructed of wood thatched with straw and measured 23 feet 6 inches by 12 feet 10 inches. The Dutch theologian Erasmus, who made several visits to Walsingham, wrote of the church that was built over the house to protect it: "Our Lady does not occupy the Priory Church. She cedes it out of deference to her Son." Erasmus also described how the jewels, gold, and silver that adorned the interior of the house glittered in candlelight. The offerings were supposed to include a phial of the Virgin's milk from Nazareth, which, some suspect, was simply chalk mixed with water. Eventually a statue of the Virgin Mary was installed in the Holy House, and it, too, became an object of devotion.

After the house was erected, chapels and crosses appeared along the road to Walsingham. About a mile south of town, a fourteenth-century chapel became known as the Slipper Chapel, for here pilgrims removed their shoes to walk the rest of the distance barefoot.

In the Middle Ages devotion to the Blessed Virgin Mary was so strong in the British Isles that England was known as Mary's Dowry. Although many other holy sites existed, Walsingham was the first great shrine to Mary in the Christian world; throughout Europe, it was believed that the broad band of stars known as the Milky Way

led there. A long line of English kings made pilgrimages to Walsingham. Among them were Edward I, who believed that Our Lady of Walsingham had intervened to save him when a large stone falling from a vaulted ceiling just missed him, and Henry VIII, who made three pilgrimages there before he broke with Rome in 1534 and placed himself at the head of the Church of England.

In the destruction of Catholic shrines and monasteries that followed, Walsingham's Holy House and the church that enclosed it were destroyed and the treasury plundered; in 1539 the statue of Mary was burned.

But the Walsingham story did not end with destruction. In the 1920s, an Anglican priest, Alfred Hope Patten, rebuilt the Holy House and the church over it and re-created the statue of Mary. Patten was guided by the Walsingham seal, now in the British Museum, which has been called "one of the most delicate and beautiful medieval representations [of Walsingham]." The Slipper Chapel, which had escaped the ravages of the Reformation, became the Roman Catholic National Shrine of Our Lady; a modern Chapel of Reconciliation is beside it. Anglicans, Roman Catholics, and members of the Eastern Orthodox Church all worship there. ❧

A Chapel for Mary
Thetford, England, c. 1104

When a community of monks from the priory at Lewes, England, moved to a new monastery at Thetford in the year 1104, they took with them a statue of the Virgin Mary and installed it over the high altar of their new church. Soon, however, a new image replaced it and it was relegated to an obscure corner of the church, an arrangement, as legend has it, that was not pleasing to Mary.

According to a narrative left by one of the monks, one night the Virgin Mary appeared to a Thetford laborer, who had been praying to her for relief from his ailments. She told him to instruct the local prior to build a chapel in her honor on the north side of the choir. The prior told the man that he agreed but, for one reason or another, he delayed construction on the project. Then the Virgin appeared to a Thetford woman and ordered her to get the prior started. However, when the woman did nothing, the Virgin appeared to her again and—to punish her for her neglect—touched her arm, causing her to lose the use of it. (The woman was cured when, on the advice of a monk, she made an offering of a wax arm to the Virgin.)

The chapel eventually was built, in size, almost the equal of the choir itself, judging from the evidence remaining. The old statue of the Virgin was then ordered painted and placed at the door of the chapel. As the painter was cleaning it, he discovered under a silver plate in the head of the image a wealth of holy relics, many of them from Jerusalem, including fragments of the rock of Calvary, pieces of the Virgin's girdle, samples of earth from the sepulcher of St. John the Evangelist, and pieces of wood from the coffins of two English saints, Edmund the Martyr and Ethelreda.

Many miracles have been attributed to the statue of Mary, which was restored to its rightful place of honor in the new chapel. When a woman suddenly lost her voice, she used signs to indicate to her friends that she desired to pray before the image of Mary in the new chapel, whereupon she regained her voice after Mary appeared to her and touched her tongue. In another legend, a cart ran over and killed a three-year-old boy; when his grieving parents vowed to make a pilgrimage to Our Lady of Thetford, the child came back to life. ✖

Master of the Saint Lucy Legend (active 1480–89), Mary, Queen of Heaven, c. 1485, National Gallery of Art, Washington, D.C.

WHERE a GODDESS'S TEMPLE STOOD
MONTE VERGINE, ITALY, 1119

IN PAGAN TIMES, THERE WAS ATOP Italy's Monte Vergine a temple dedicated to Cybele, a goddess known as the mother of the gods. In 1119, Mary and the Christ Child appeared on the mountain to a hermit, St. William of Vercelli, and commanded him to build a church there honoring Mary, the true mother of God. The site was marked by a flock of pure white doves.

When William finished the chapel, he founded an order whose members lived austerely and wore white robes in honor of the Virgin's purity. The chapel eventually became part of a large basilica. Pilgrims still go there to venerate a painting said to have been done by St. Luke. Only the top half showing the heads of the Virgin and Child is original; the large painting was cut in half when it was brought to Italy from Constantinople in 1261. It was restored and repainted in 1310.

William founded other communities in Italy. When his enemies sent a prostitute to seduce him, he lay down on the hot coals of his fire and invited her to join him. Seeing that he was not burned, she was converted. St. William died in 1142 and soon became the object of a cult at Monte Vergine. ✃

OUR LADY OF GUADALUPE
MEXICO, 1531

IT WAS THE HEAVENLY SOUNDS— something like a choir of songbirds, most unusual for a cold winter day—that brought the Mexican peasant Juan Diego to a sudden stop as he ran over a hill called Tepeyac. The date was Saturday, December 9, 1531.

Then he heard a woman's voice of incomparable sweetness calling him from above: "Juan, Juan Diego, Juanito, Juan Dieguito." Climbing to the top of the rock-strewn hill, Juan beheld a beautiful Mexican girl, "radiant as the sun," emerging from a golden cloud of light. She spoke to him in his native dialect, "Juan, smallest and dearest of my little children, where were you going?" After Juan explained that he was on his way to the town of Tlaltelolco to hear Mass and receive religious instruction, the young woman identified herself: "I am the ever-virgin Mary, Mother of the true God who gives life and maintains it in existence."

The apparition asked that a church—a *trecoali* in Juan's Aztec dialect—be built on that spot and promised, "I will show my compassion to your people and to all people who sincerely ask my help in their work and in their sorrows." The Virgin then told him to go to Tenochtitlán, the native word for the settlement that was to become Mexico City, and relay her request to the bishop. Juan Diego, now prostrate on the ground before her, agreed to do this at once.

Juan Diego was then fifty-seven years old. He lived near his uncle, Juan Bernardino, who had raised him from childhood, in a nearby village called Tolpetlac. The two men had been converted to Christianity, a faith that had been brought to Mexico by Cortez during his conquest in 1519–21, just a few years before. Juan Diego knew nothing of the world beyond his own village. He had never been to Tenochtitlán, although the island city was only five miles away.

José Rafael Aragón (active 1820–62), Virgin of Guadalupe, c. 1830s, santos figure, private collection.

When Juan arrived at the palace of Fray Juan de Zumárraga, the Bishop-elect of Tenochtitlán, suspicious servants kept the rustic, who insisted that his message was for the bishop's ears only, waiting for hours. Finally Juan was ushered into the bishop's presence. No one knows exactly what was said; apparently Bishop Zumárraga humored Juan Diego by promising he would think about the Virgin's request for a church at Tepeyac and he ended the interview on an encouraging note: he said that Juan Diego could return later if he wanted.

Juan was not happy about the message he had to relay to the Virgin, who was waiting for him in the same place on the hill. He implored her to send someone else, insisting, "I am nobody." But the Virgin was not to be dissuaded. Addressing him as "my little son," she replied: "There are many I could send. But you are the one I have chosen." She told him to return the next day to the bishop and repeat the request.

At the palace on Sunday, the bishop again listened patiently,

then told Juan to ask the Virgin for a sign as proof of who she was. Back at Tepeyac, the Virgin told her "little son" to return the next morning and she would provide a sign.

Juan returned home to find his uncle deathly ill with fever. To nurse him, Juan stayed by his bedside and did not meet the Virgin, as he had promised, on Monday morning. On Tuesday, his uncle implored Juan to go to Tlaltelolco for a priest. Juan set off immediately, but, in crossing Tepeyac, he veered around the other side of the hill in hopes of avoiding the Virgin. But, as he had feared, there she was, blocking his path.

Juan was afraid the Virgin would be angry, but she reassured him: "Do not be distressed and afraid." His uncle had already recovered from his illness, she said. Now Juan was free to go on to the bishop and repeat her request that a church be built. But first he needed a sign, so she sent him to the top of the mountain to pick the flowers growing there.

Juan Diego must have wondered what sort of flowers he would find growing there among the cacti in the middle of December. But there they were —Castilian roses growing in profusion. He made a pouch from his *tilma*, the traditional blanket-like cape he was wear-

ing, filled it with blossoms, and hurried back to where the Virgin waited. She neatly rearranged the flowers, tied the lower corners of the *tilma* around his neck so the flowers wouldn't fall out, and sent him on his way with the promise that, this time, the bishop would believe him.

At the palace, Juan came before the bishop and members of his entourage. He told his story, then untied the cape and let the flowers tumble to the floor. But it wasn't the winter roses that caused the bishop and others to fall to their knees. It was the cape. For there on the outside of the rough woven garment was a picture of Mary, just as Juan Diego had described her: a radiant figure bathed in golden rays of light, wearing a bluish mantle bordered in gold and adorned with golden stars.

The next day, Wednesday, the *tilma* was taken to the cathedral where crowds came to see and worship. Juan took the bishop to the spot where he first saw the Virgin and then returned to his village, where his uncle was waiting, completely cured. He told Juan that while he was near death, a young woman, surrounded by a soft light, appeared out of the darkness and told him that she had sent his nephew to Tenochtitlán with a picture of herself. Just before she vanished, she said, "Call me and

Rufino Tamayo (1899–1991), The Virgin of Guadalupe, 1926, Mary-Anne Martin/Fine Art, New York City.

call my image Santa María de Guadalupe." When the Spanish clergy heard that, they were delighted, for Guadalupe, in that era, was the name of the most famous shrine to Mary in Spain.

It took only thirteen days to build a simple chapel at the site. On the day after Christmas, a procession brought the *tilma* to Tepeyac. Until he died in 1548, Juan Diego lived in a hut next to the chapel, where he spent his days telling his story and showing the picture on the cape to pilgrims. After his uncle died in 1544, his simple dwelling in Tolpetlac became a chapel.

The Virgin's image continued to work miracles. In 1544, the presence of the *tilma* is believed to have ended a pestilence that was decimating the population of Mexico City. In 1546, when heavy rains threatened to flood the city, a lay sister dreamed she saw the Virgin of Guadalupe propping up the walls of the convent, and so the picture was returned to Mexico City until the waters subsided. In 1921, with the *tilma* now in a large cathedral at Tepeyac, anticlerical forces detonated a powerful bomb that was hidden in flowers at the altar. The blast miraculously killed no one and caused no damage to the image of Mary.

There have been many scientific inquiries into the structure of the *tilma,* including one in 1977 that used infrared photography and computer enhancement to examine the picture, but none has produced a satisfactory explanation of how an image of such startling clarity could be superimposed on material woven from crude cactus cloth. Under ordinary circumstances, such material should have disintegrated within twenty years. Nor has the cloth been sized or the paint varnished, but still the image has not faded or cracked in more than four and a half centuries. The artists and scientists who have examined the Virgin of Guadalupe over the years mostly agree with the inquiry of 1666 that concluded, "it is impossible for any human craftsman to paint or create a work so fine, clean, and well-formed on a fabric so coarse as that of this *tilma.*"

It is also believed that the name Guadalupe might have been the result of linguistic confusion—or perhaps it was divine design. In speaking to the uncle, Juan Bernardino, in dialect, the Virgin might have used a word, *Coatlallope,* that sounded like Guadalupe to the Spaniards but to the natives meant "who treads on the snake." The Spaniards were pleased because the word, as they heard it, linked the miracle at Tepeyac to the most famous shrine to Mary in Spain, and the natives were delighted because the word in their language predicted the demise of a dreaded god, a feathered serpent, whom they would happily be rid of.

The Virgin of Guadalupe helped the Mexican people achieve a national and religious identity. In 1754, Pope Benedict XIV declared her Patroness and Protectress of New Spain, and during the Mexican Revolutionary Wars, the insurgents rallied to the cry "Long live the Virgin of Guadalupe and down with bad government." And they carried her image on their banners into battle.

Today, the influence of the Virgin of Guadalupe is felt throughout the hemisphere, especially in the southwestern United States. In 1945, she was again coronated, this time as "Queen of Wisdom of the Americas."

At Tepeyac the original chapel holding the *tilma* was rebuilt several times until it was replaced by a twin-towered basilica in 1709. The *tilma* was moved again in 1976 to a new, round cathedral, built next to the old, with a capacity of ten thousand people. Twelve million people visit Guadalupe, long ago swallowed up by Mexico City, every year. It is, by far, the most popular shrine to the Virgin Mary in the Western Hemisphere. ⚮

A CHAPEL IN RUINS
LE LAUS, FRANCE, 1664

IN MAY 1664, BENOÎTE RENCUREL, a seventeen-year-old shepherd, was tending her flock of sheep on a mountain in the French Alps named for the third-century martyr St. Maurice. She had just sat down in a meadow to have lunch and say her rosary, when an old man in a red robe appeared and introduced himself as none other than St. Maurice himself. When the girl said she was thirsty, he pointed to a spring—one that she had never seen before— that was flowing out of the ground at her side. He told her to take her sheep the next day to graze nearer her home in St. Etienne. It was here, while standing on a rock known as Les Fours, that she first beheld the Virgin Mary with the Christ Child, an apparition that appeared to her regularly for the next two months.

Eventually, Benoîte asked the Lady who she was. "I am Mary, the Mother of Jesus," she replied, adding, "It is the will of my Son that I should be honored in this parish, though not

on this spot." A month later, the Virgin appeared to Benoîte amid a light "shining brighter than the sun." "Go to Le Laus," she told the shepherd girl. "There you will find a little chapel where delicious perfumes abound. There you will often find and see me."

The chapel in Le Laus was practically in ruins, but it was the Virgin's desire that it be rebuilt and enshrined in a larger church, with funding given by the poor. "I have requested Le Laus from my Divine Son for the conversion of sinners and He has given it to me," Mary told Benoîte. "Many sinners will be converted here." But before work started on the church, Benoîte was subjected to rigorous questioning by ecclesiastical authorities. Their doubts about the authenticity of the appari-

tions were dispelled when a local woman, crippled and helpless for years, regained her health and the use of her limbs while worshipping at the chapel.

The first donation for the church, a sum large enough to get the work started, was a gold coin, a *louis d'or*, that was given by a woman dressed in rags. From that point on, there was always just enough money for the next day's work on hand. The church was completed in four years. In it, there is a statue of the Virgin as she appeared to Benoîte. A lamp burns in front of a shrine dedicated to Mary; the oil from it is said to have cured the sick and the lame. Benoîte Rencurel is buried in a vault in front of the high altar. She died "in the odor of sanctity 18 December, 1718," the inscription reads. ✂

MARY'S BRIDGE OF ICE
CAP-DE-LA-MADELEINE, QUEBEC, 1879

Gentile da Fabriano (1370–1427), Coronation of the Virgin, *1420s, Collection of the J. Paul Getty Museum, Malibu, California.*

THE SEVENTEENTH-CENTURY SETtlement named Cap-de-la-Madeleine is located on the north bank of the St. Lawrence River about midway between Montreal and Quebec City. At this site, in 1662, Jesuit fathers built a chapel dedicated to the Virgin Mary, and in 1694 Canada's first Confraternity of the Holy Rosary was founded there.

Over the years, however, attendance at the chapel fell off considerably. In 1867 a priest sent to revitalize the parish found not one person in church on the eve of the feast of the Ascension; instead he saw a pig wandering inside the empty chapel, a rosary in its mouth. The priest, Father Luc Desilets, made "The Pig and the Rosary" the subject of his sermon the next day, and from that point on, the parishioners, shamed by their neglect of their religious duties, became more active in the parish and the numbers of people attending services increased until soon a new church was needed.

For two years stone for a new building was cut in a quarry across the St. Lawrence River. The plan was to haul the building material across when the river froze, but weather that winter of 1879 was exceptionally mild and no ice formed. So Father Desilets prayed to the Virgin Mary for a bridge of ice strong enough to hold the weight of the stone. In return, he promised her to leave the original 1662 church alone and not to take stone from it, as he had planned, for the new church.

The priest's prayers were answered immediately. On March 15 gale-force winds began to pile up ice floes until, the next morning, there was a bridge of ice spanning the river, strong enough to bear the weight of the stone sleds. It took a week to haul the stone across the bridge. Then a thaw set in, the weather became mild again, and the frozen bridge melted away.

The new church opened on October 3, 1880. The original chapel was also restored and consecrated to the Virgin Mary in 1888. Later the same year, Father Desilets and a new priest, Father Frédéric, were praying in the chapel when they observed that a statue of the Virgin Mary in front of them raised her eyes from the usual downcast position and, with eyes open, stared straight ahead. The statue, which has been known as Our Lady of the Holy Rosary ever since it was donated to the Confraternity in the mid-nineteenth century, raised her eyes, Father Desilets later wrote, "and looked in front of her as if looking outwards, far into the distance. Her face was at times severe and sometimes sad."

In the early twentieth century, Our Lady of the Holy Rosary became the first Madonna to be crowned, by order of the Pope, in Canada and it remains the only one. Pope John Paul II visited the shrine, which is the most popular of those dedicated to Mary in Canada, in 1984. The complex at Cap-de-la-Madeleine, now called Notre Dame du Cap, now includes a monastery and convent, a perpetual adoration chapel, a retreat house and other accommodations for pilgrims, and a Stations of the Cross which is reached by the Rosary Bridge across a stream that feeds the St. Lawrence River. ❧

Luis Niño (active c. 1730–50), Our Lady of the Victory of Málaga (detail), c. 1735, Denver Art Museum.

Lady of the Helping Hand

MARY HAS A BENEVOLENT HABIT of stepping into situations when people are in danger or in need. In 1527, she stopped a horde of marauding German soldiers advancing on the Italian town of Frascati with a spoken warning: "Back, soldiers! This land is mine." The martial name of the oldest statue of Mary in the United States, *La Conquistadora,* dates back to when the statue supposedly aided the Spaniards in their reconquest of New Mexico, beginning in 1692. The American victory in the Battle of New Orleans in 1815 has been attributed to another famous Marian image, Our Lady of Prompt Succor.

Our Lady of Czestochowa is a black Madonna, a painting on which the title Queen of Poland has been bestowed. She has come to the aid of the Polish people several times, but, long before the painting arrived in Poland, it was treasured in Constantinople where it was given credit for warding off an attack by Moslems.

There are countless stories in which Mary comes to the aid of individuals. One example involves a blind beggar who in 457 was rescued by a Greek soldier after the poor man had wandered off the road leading to Constantinople. Both men called on the Virgin to help them. She not only did, she also rewarded them handsomely for their devotion to her, a happy ending that is characteristic of so many miracle stories.

Canadian, 18th century, Ex-voto of Monsieur Roger, *1717, Basilique Sainte-Anne-de-Beaupré, Quebec.*

THE EMPEROR AND THE BLIND MAN
CONSTANTINOPLE, 457

AT HIGH NOON, IN THE YEAR 457, a blind beggar named Simeon was making his way along a hot and dusty road near Constantinople, when the old dog that was guiding him collapsed from the heat. The old man tried to go on alone, but he soon strayed from the road and began wandering through the wilderness, perilously close to the edges of cliffs and unseen quagmires of quicksand. When he could continue no longer, he fell to the ground and cried: "Holy Virgin! I have always had confidence in your protection. Do not let me perish here without succor."

Soon the blind man heard the footsteps of a young Greek soldier named Leo who was carrying dispatches to Constantinople. Simeon called out: "In the name of Jesus our Savior, in the name of the Virgin His Mother, if you are a Christian, save blind Simeon! Leave me not here to die." As Leo, a valiant and compassionate man, led Simeon back to the road, the beggar explained that he was on his way to Constantinople, where, the Virgin had promised in a dream, his sight would be restored so he could see the new emperor.

"What!" said Leo. "Is the Emperor Marcian dead?"

"I know not," Simeon replied. "Only that the Virgin has told me that I shall see the crowning of the new emperor."

By this time Simeon was so thirsty he could go no farther, so Leo left him in the shade of some trees and went off to find water. When he found only dried-up pools, he called upon "the Queen of Heaven" for aid: "This unfortunate man has exposed himself to these dangers because he trusted in thee. Do not permit his faith to prove deceptive."

Then, just as he was about to give up the search, he heard a voice: "Leo, why are you so troubled, while just before you is a pond full of water?" Leo found the pond but he was still worried that he might be too late to save the old man. The voice reassured him: "Fear not. She whom the blind man invoked will not abandon him in his suffering."

And the voice went on to tell Leo: "And because your soul is compassionate and your heart open to the appeal of the unfortunate, and because you have confidence in my intercession, and have honored me with a persevering devotion, I have obtained for you the highest earthly dignity man can seek. You will be proclaimed Emperor,

Ethiopian, after 1600, Our Lady Mary with Her Beloved Son (triptych, center panel), Institute of Ethiopian Studies, Addis Ababa.

OBSIDIO CLARI MONTIS CZĘSTOCHOVIENSIS.
DEIPARÆ IMAGINEA.D. LVCÆ DE PICTÆ IN REGNO POLONIÆ

Ab Exercitu Suecorum, Duce Burch ardo Mellero Generali Legato.
Authore STANISLAO A ROBIERZYCKO Robie
DANTISCI Sumptibus GEORGII FORSTERI, S.R.M. Bibliopola. Aº 1659.

and you shall sit on the throne where sat Constantine, my servant; and you shall reign with glory during seventeen years."

She also told Leo to fill his helmet with water and to take a handful of mud. "You shall give the water to the old man to drink and he shall regain his strength; and you shall anoint his eyes, and he shall see."

Leo did as the voice commanded him, and when the old man had regained his strength and his sight, they both thanked the Virgin Mary. Then they proceeded on to Constantinople, where, as the Virgin had foretold, Leo was made Emperor of the Byzantine Empire. He reigned until his death seventeen years later. ❧

BLACK MADONNA
CZESTOCHOWA, POLAND, 1382

ACCORDING TO LEGEND, LUKE THE Evangelist, the patron saint of artists, painted the image of the Virgin Mary and Christ Child that has been venerated since the Middle Ages as Our Lady of Czestochowa, Poland. For his canvas, St. Luke is believed to have used the wooden top of a table that was built by the carpenter Jesus. After the Crucifixion, Mary took the table with her when she went to live with St. John. It was there, in St. John's home, that Mary sat for St. Luke. While he painted her, she told him stories about the life of Christ that he later used in his gospel. The work is one of a number of famous so-called Black Madonnas, statues and paintings that depict Mary as a black or dark-complexioned woman, an interpretation possibly inspired by a passage in the Song of Songs:

"I am black, but comely, O ye daughters of Jerusalem."

In the fourth century, the Empress Helena, the energetic collector of Christian relics, discovered the painting in Jerusalem and took it to her son, the Emperor Constantine in Constantinople, who built a church for it. The first of many miracles attributed to the painting occurred here, when the citizens paraded the image through the streets to fend off—successfully, as the story goes—the attacks of the Saracens.

After five hundred years or so in Constantinople, the painting turned up in Poland, where it became, in the fourteenth century, the property of the Polish prince Ladislaus. In 1382, as invading Tatars attacked the prince's castle in Belz, an arrow flew through a window and

Virgin of Czestochowa, *engraving from* Obsidio clari montis Czestochoviensis, *by Stanislaus Kobierzycki, Danzig, 1659.*

struck the Virgin of the painting in the throat. Ladislaus then fled with the painting, and, in his flight, stopped for the night at Czestochowa, where the painting was installed temporarily in a small church. The next morning he put the painting back in the carriage, but when his horse refused to move, the prince took it as a sign that God wished the painting to remain there. He then had a Pauline monastery and church built to ensure the painting's safety.

In 1430, Hussites, followers of the Czech reformer John Huss, overran the monastery and attempted to make off with the portrait of the Virgin. In the fracas, one of the looters struck the painting twice with his sword, but before he could do any other damage, he fell writhing in agony and died. The two sword cuts on the Virgin's cheek—and the wound on her throat caused by the arrow—are visible to this day.

In 1566, the monks successfully defended the monastery and the holy image of Mary for forty days against the forces of Charles X of Sweden. After that the Lady of Czestochowa became a symbol of national unity and was crowned Queen of Poland. There is also a legend that, on September 14, 1920, the Russian Army, which had gathered on the banks of the Vistula River threatening Warsaw, withdrew after the

Attributed to Giovanni Antonio Vanoni (1810–1886), Ex-voto from the Oratory of the "Poss," Golino, Switzerland, Ufficio dei Musei Etnografici, Giubiasco, Switzerland.

image of the Virgin appeared in the clouds over the city.

In a historic visit by a Pope to a Communist-controlled country, John Paul II, a native son, visited the Lady of Czestochowa in 1979, shortly after being elected pontiff. ⌘

A Voice Against the Enemy
Frascati, Italy, 1527

To punish Pope Clement VII for allying himself with Francis I of France, Emperor Charles V, in 1527, sent German troops, most of them Lutherans, into southern Italy, where they sacked Rome and imprisoned the Pope. They then began pillaging the surrounding towns and villages. On Sunday, May 1, they advanced on Frascati, eleven miles southeast of Rome, a town with famous vineyards but no way of defending itself against the onslaught. When the soldiers reached the entrance to the town, however, a voice boomed out over the commotion of the advancing army: "Back, soldiers! This land is mine." The command threw the invaders into total confusion and they fled the town in terror.

The voice had come from a fresco depicting the Virgin and Child that adorned a wall surrounding a vineyard. The painting had never attracted any particular notice before, but after it repulsed the attackers, it became the center of attention in the town and the source of other legends and miracles.

To protect the painting, the town built a chapel over it, a structure that soon proved too small to hold all the pilgrims drawn to Frascati by news of the miracle. In 1611, a wealthy priest named Jerome de Rossi-Cavoletti was celebrating Mass, when, to his distress, the host disappeared from his hands. When he could not find it, he beseeched the Virgin for help and heard, within himself, a voice saying, "Jerome, you are rich in the goods of this world. Look at this humble chapel. Is it worthy of the Queen of Heaven?" The father immediately vowed to build a larger and more beautiful church and the host reappeared on the altar.

A century later, in 1713, the Virgin came to the aid of the town again, when, during a crowded church service, the painting cried out: "Flee! Flee!" The worshipers rushed from the church just before the roof caved in. In 1796, the Virgin of the painting was seen alternately to open and close her eyes, an action that the devout interpreted in two ways: by closing her eyes, the Virgin was shutting out the iniquity of the world; by opening them again, she was bestowing her compassion on mankind.

During World War II, the Germans were headquartered in Frascati, and the town suffered much damage from Allied bombing. Fortunately, the painting had been removed from the church and stored safely elsewhere before bombs destroyed the church. Construction of another church to house the painting was completed in 1954. ✑

LA CONQUISTADORA
SANTA FE, NEW MEXICO, 1693

THE WOODEN STATUE, THIRTY-one-inches-high, known as *La Conquistadora* is the oldest such image of the Virgin Mary in North America. In 1625, a famous Spanish missionary, Friar Alonso de Benavides, took her from Mexico City by wagon train to Santa Fe, a settlement that had been founded only fifteen years before. Four years later she was enthroned in her own chapel. At that point in her history, she was known as Our Lady of the Assumption.

On August 10, 1680, the Indians of the New Mexican pueblos rebelled, killing twenty-one friars and several families living outside of Santa Fe. In town, more than one thousand civilians and soldiers took refuge in the walled Palace of the Governors, where they were besieged for eleven days. On August 21, in a dramatic episode in Santa Fe's history, the Spaniards fought their way out of the settlement and fled south to El Paso. The statue of Mary was carried to safety by the wife of a Spanish captain.

In 1692, Don Diego de Vargas, known as the Peaceful Reconqueror, led another force of Spaniards into New Mexico to put down the Indian rebellion and claim the land for Spain. Vargas, a pious Spanish nobleman, wanted to accomplish his mission without bloodshed; he ordered his men to sing the praises of the Virgin as they approached a rebel pueblo. He also vowed to honor the Virgin every year if the reconquest was peaceful and to rebuild the chapel that was destroyed in the Pueblo Revolt of 1680.

Through diplomacy—and a show of force—the Spaniards reached Santa Fe without having to fight. But the next year, when Vargas returned with settlers

—and *La Conquistadora*—he had to use force to evict the Indians from the settlement. Ever since the Spanish reconquest, the statue, which Santa Feans have traditionally turned to in times of trouble, has been known as *La Conquistadora,* or Our Lady of the Conquest. In 1769, her aid was invoked in combating a threat by Comanche Indians, after a member of one of Santa Fe's oldest and most prominent families was killed in a skirmish with them. *La Conquistadora* was named Patroness of New Mexico at the same time.

Diego de Vargas kept his promise to honor *La Conquistadora* annually; each year in early June she is taken in a procession from the Cathedral of St. Francis, where she occupies a side chapel, to the Rosario, a chapel built about 1800. The church that Vargas promised, however, was not built until 1714. The present-day Cathedral of St. Francis was built around it in the early nineteenth century.

In 1960, as part of the celebration of the 350th anniversary of the founding of Santa Fe, *La Conquistadora* was crowned by order of Pope John XXIII. (To qualify for a coronation, a statue must have been venerated for at least three hundred years.) In 1973, *La Conquistadora* was stolen from the cathedral. The statue was recovered in an abandoned mine shaft in the Manzano Mountains. ༄

MARY SAVES A CITY
NEW ORLEANS, 1812 AND 1815

WHEN, IN 1808, MOTHER ST. Michel, a noted educator of the Ursuline order in France, received a request from the order's convent in New Orleans that she join them in their educational and charitable endeavors, she applied to her bishop for permission to go to America. He did not want to lose her, however, so he said she must receive permission to leave from the Pope. But, as the bishop well knew, the Pope, Pius VII, was at that time literally a prisoner of Napoleon in Rome, cut off from all communication with the outside world.

Mother St. Michel wrote to the Pope anyway and invoked divine assistance, praying: "O most holy Virgin Mary, if you obtain a prompt and favorable answer to my letter, I promise to have you honored in New Orleans under the title of Our Lady of Prompt Succor." She sent the letter on March 19, 1809, and within six

Sandro Botticelli (1445–1510), The Annunciation (detail), Uffizi Gallery.

weeks had a favorable response from the pontiff. Mother St. Michel had a statue of Our Lady of Prompt Succor carved and took it with her on the voyage to New Orleans. There, after she landed on December 31, 1810, the image of Mary was installed in the convent's chapel.

Numerous favors have been attributed to Our Lady of Prompt Succor. The history of the convent states: "Under this new title the Blessed Virgin has so often manifested her power and goodness, that the religious repose in her an unbounded confidence." One of the notable favors was bestowed in 1812 when an immense fire ravaging the city threatened to destroy the convent. The nuns were about to abandon the building, when a lay sister placed the statue of Mary in a window facing the flames and Mother St. Michel implored the Virgin: "Our Lady of Prompt Succor, we are lost if you come not to our help." At this moment the wind changed direction and the convent was saved from the flames.

Three years later, as the War of 1812 was coming to an end, the convent was again in peril: British forces intent on plundering the city attacked New Orleans on January 8, 1815. During the battle, which took place in the swamps and canefields south of the city, women gathered in the convent to pray, and members of the Ursuline community vowed to have a Mass of Thanksgiving sung every year if the Americans were victorious. When news of the overwhelming American victory—more than two thousand British casualties against eight Americans killed and thirteen wounded—reached the convent, a *Te Deum*, a traditional hymn of Thanksgiving, was sung. The American general, Andrew Jackson, who was a Protestant, later went to the convent to thank the nuns in person for their prayers.

General Jackson also wrote the priest who had conducted the Mass of Thanksgiving: "The signal interposition of Heaven in giving success to our arms requires some external manifestation of the feelings of our most lively gratitude. Permit me, therefore, to entreat that you will cause the service of public thanksgiving to be performed in the cathedral, in token of the great assistance we have received from the Ruler of all events, and of our humble sense of it."

In November 1895, by decree of Pope Leo XIII, Our Lady of Prompt Succor was crowned; in 1928 she was named the principal patroness of the City of New Orleans and of the State of Louisiana. ⚘

English, 12th century, Virgin and Child, manuscript illumination, Bodleian Library, Oxford.

Mary's Gifts

MARY OFTEN GIVES GIFTS to her visionaries that become objects of devotion for mankind. In 1326, she told a cowherd where to find a carved image of herself that had been buried for over six hundred years; this statue made Guadalupe, Spain, into a major Christian shrine. The century before, there was a gift from Mary on an even grander scale. The house in which she was born in Nazareth—and where the angel Gabriel announced that she would become the mother of God—was transported by angels from Nazareth and deposited in Loreto, Italy. In the 1700s, an invisible Mary guided the hand of an artist to produce her likeness on canvas; it is now enshrined in León, Mexico.

In 1208, Mary gave St. Dominic the prayer beads known as the rosary, called by the Church "a singular remedy against heresy and sin." Soon afterward, in 1251, she bestowed a similar talisman on St. Simon Stock in England: the brown scapular, two pieces of material that are worn hung over the shoulders, front and back. The scapular is, in Mary's words, "the badge of salvation, a shield in time of danger and a pledge of special peace and protection." The Miraculous Medal, worn by many Catholics, is modeled on a vision that the nun Catherine Labouré had of the Virgin Mary in 1830. Countless cures, conversions, and other miracles have been attributed to the medal.

Mario Parial (Philippines, b. 1945), Our Lady of Mt. Carmel/Nuestra Señora del Carmen *(detail), Dr. and Mrs. Yolando Sulit Collection.*

St. Dominic and the Rosary
Prouille, France, 1208

Five years before he had a vision of the Virgin Mary, Dominic (Domingo) de Guzmán went from his native Spain into southern France to oppose heretics who were spreading their doctrine throughout that part of the country. In a story that has come down through the centuries, a document written by Dominic was cast into a fire three times to test the truth of his argument. Instead of burning, the treatise flew out of the fire each time. Meanwhile, a paper composed by an heretical opponent was totally consumed by the flames.

St. Dominic (c. 1170–1221) founded the Order of Friars Preachers, commonly called Dominicans, in Prouille, France, with the mission of saving souls, primarily through preaching. Legend has it that St. Dominic was inspired to found the order when his preaching converted the keeper of an inn where he was staying. The order received final papal approval in 1216.

One of St. Dominic's favorite prayers was the Hail Mary, for, a commentator wrote, "no name after that of our Lord was so welcome to him as that sweet name of Mary, or so often on his lips." In 1208, while he was praying to Mary in the chapel of Notre Dame in Prouille, she appeared to him and gave him the rosary, urging him to explain its use to the people. As an official Church account states: "He was admonished by the Blessed Virgin to preach the Rosary to the people as a singular remedy against heresy and sin."

Perhaps the best description of the apparition is contained in an undated poem written by a Dominican Sister:

> *H*e knelt, his lips apart,
>   his heart aflame;
>   While Mary taught,
> the angels went and came.
> "Take it," she said with love,
>   "this Rosary."
>   Her God! her Son,
> she held upon her knee.
>   His hand He raised—
> the mystic chaplet blessed.
>   With rapture, Dominic,
>   his joy expressed.

Scholars today consider the story of the rosary and St. Dominic's apparition to be legend, not fact, but that has not always been the case. In 1891, Pope Leo XIII affirmed his belief in the story: "The belief that to this form of prayer a special power has been accorded by the Queen of Heaven is justified, because by her instigation and under her patronage it was

Caravaggio (1571–1610), Madonna of the Rosary with Saint Dominic and Saint Peter Martyr, 1607, Kunsthistorisches Museum, Vienna.

introduced by the holy Father Dominic, and it was spread in a time hostile to everything Catholic, much like our own, and as a powerful means of opposing the enemies of the faith effectually." Dominic was canonized in 1234, soon after his death. ⚭

SIMON STOCK'S BADGE, PLEDGE, AND SHIELD
CAMBRIDGE, ENGLAND, 1251

ALTHOUGH LITTLE IS KNOWN about Simon Stock's early life, legend has it that the name, Stock, meaning "tree trunk," derives from the fact that, beginning at age twelve, he lived as a hermit in the hollow trunk of an oak tree. It is also believed that, as a young man, he went on a pilgrimage to the Holy Land where he joined a group of Carmelites with whom he later returned to Europe. Simon Stock founded many Carmelite communities, especially in university towns such as Cambridge, Oxford, Paris, and Bologna, and he helped to change the Carmelites from a hermit order to one of mendicant friars. In 1254 he was elected superior-general of his order at London.

Simon Stock's lasting fame came from an apparition he had in Cambridge, England, on July 16, 1251, at a time when the Carmelite order was being oppressed. In it the Virgin Mary appeared to him holding the brown scapular in one hand. Her words were: "Receive, my beloved son, this scapular of thy order; it is the special sign of my favor, which I have obtained for thee and for thy children of Mount Carmel. He who dies clothed with this habit shall be preserved from eternal fire. It is the badge of salvation, a shield in time of danger, and a pledge of special peace and protection."

The scapular (from the Latin, *scapula*, meaning "shoulder blade") consists of two pieces of cloth, one worn on the chest, the other on the back, which are connected by straps or strings passing over the shoulders. In certain orders, monks and nuns wear scapulars that reach from the shoulders almost to the ground as outer garments. Lay persons usually wear scapulars underneath their clothing; these consist of two pieces of material only a few inches square.

There are elaborate rules governing the wearing of the scapular: although it may be worn by any Catholic, even an infant, the investiture must be done by a priest. And the scapular must be worn in the proper manner; if an individual neglects to wear it

Mexican, late 19th century, Our Lady of Mt. Carmel/ Nuestra Señora de Carmen, *retablo, private collection.*

for a time, the benefits are forfeited. The Catholic Church has approved eighteen different kinds of scapulars of which the best known is the woolen brown scapular, or Scapular of Mount Carmel, that the Virgin Mary bestowed on Simon Stock. ⌒

No Place More Holy
Loreto, Italy, 1294

In 1295, unseen hands put down the Holy House of Nazareth in the middle of an ancient road near Loreto, Italy. Also known as the House of the Angelic Salutation, this is where Mary was born, where the angel Gabriel announced to her that she was to become the mother of God, and where Jesus Christ lived as a child. The story of the miraculous flight of the house from the Holy Land to Italy has received, writes H. M. Gillette, an authority on the shrines of Europe, "the ridicule of one half of the world and the devotion of the other."

Loreto, however, was not the first stop. Three and a half years earlier, on May 10, 1291, shepherds discovered the same house in a field in Dalmatia at Tersatto, where no house had ever stood. After the local parish priest, who had seen the Holy House in a vision, identified it, the governor of Dalmatia sent a delegation to Nazareth. It reported back that the Holy House, which had been covered by the Basilica of the Annuncia-

tion, was gone, and its foundation, which remained, matched the 15-by-30-foot house exactly. What's more, the house was built from limestone and cedarwood, materials that were not found in that part of Dalmatia.

When it was mysteriously taken from Dalmatia, the Holy House was first deposited, on December 10, 1294, in a laurel wood near Loreto, where the trees seemed bent over in permanent bows of respect. Robbers took to attacking pilgrims in this remote spot, however, so the same "angelic hands" soon transported the house to the middle of Loreto, on the high road to Recanati, where it may be seen today.

As it appeared in Loreto, the house—the Santa Casa—held only an altar, a hearth, and a statue of the Virgin Mary on a pedestal beside the altar. The house had a single door and, beside that, a small window. The ceiling was painted blue and spangled with gold stars. Pope Clement VII (1523–34) added more doors to accommodate

"De Beatissimo B. Mariae Virginis Sacello Lauretano," engraving from Vita Beatae Mariae Virginis, Cologne, 1592, Spencer Collection, New York Public Library.

the crowds of pilgrims and placed the statue in a niche lined with jewels.

The house itself has been much examined. An excavation ordered by Pope Benedict XIV (1740–58) proved that there was no foundation and that the house rested directly on the ancient road. Later examinations have shown that the mortar and stones in the walls are identical with those in the foundation at Nazareth. The same experts determined that the walls of the house were original and that the structure had never been rebuilt.

Ever since it appeared in Loreto, the house has been a popular destination for pilgrims, among them Dalmatians lamenting the loss of the house from their land. The Santuario della Santa Casa, a church with a fortress-like exterior, was built to enclose and protect the Holy House. Construction began in 1468 under Pope Paul II; the Holy House is located under the dome of the Santuario, which dates from 1500. Pope Julius II approved the Holy House as a place of pilgrimage in 1510, the same year that Donato Bramante designed the high marble screen around the Santa Casa.

In 1936, by papal decree, the house was granted indulgences equal to those of Lourdes and the Holy Land. Visiting pilgrims are admonished by an inscription:

Let those who are impure tremble to enter into this sanctuary. The whole world has not a place more sacred. . . . For here was the Word made Flesh, and here was born the Virgin Mother. From the West, where the sun goes down, to the East, where it rises from the waters, no place is more holy. ☙

SIX HUNDRED YEARS BURIED IN A CAVE
GUADALUPE, SPAIN, 1326

OUR LADY OF GUADALUPE IS A richly decorated statue made of dark wood, a so-called black virgin. It was given in the year 580 by Pope Gregory the Great to Bishop Leander of Seville in Spain. During the Moorish invasion of 711, when the priests of Seville fled north, they took the statue with them. A fifteenth-century account says that when they came to the mountains near the Guadalupe River, "the saintly priests dug a cave that was like a tomb, surrounded the cave with large boulders, and placed inside it the image of our lady Saint Mary."

The statue was lost and forgotten during the long struggle

Mexican, late 19th century, Our Lady of the Holy Cave/ Nuestra Señora de la Cueva Santa, retablo, private collection.

by Christian forces to take Spain back from the Moors. The expulsion of the Moors was largely complete when, in 1326, a cowherd named Gil Cordero found one of his cows lying dead near a spring. As he started to butcher it, opening its breast in the traditional way with a cut in the form of a cross, the cow, to the herdsman's astonishment and fear, stood up very much alive. Then the Virgin Mary appeared and said to him: "Have no fear, for I am the mother of God by whom the human race achieved redemption. Take your cow and go . . . to your home and tell the clergy and other people to come to this place where I appear to you and to dig here, and they will find a statue of me."

The herdsman did as he was told, and when others mocked him, he convinced them he was telling the truth by pointing to the cow and saying, "Friends, do not dismiss these things; if you will not believe me, then believe the mark the cow bears on her breast." And he told the clergy where to dig to find the statue, adding that the Virgin also told him that "she would have many people come to her house from many regions because of the many miracles she would work on sea as well as land." So the clergy and others went there and found the statue of Mary just where it had been buried some six hundred years before.

The clergy immediately began building a crude chapel to house the Madonna; later the King of Spain ordered that a chapel be built on the site, which soon became a shrine. Over the centuries, members of the ruling class donated elaborate garments for the statue, including a headdress containing thirty thousand jewels. It is believed that Christopher Columbus prayed here before making his first voyage to the New World, where he named a West Indian island Guadeloupe in honor of the Virgin. ⁒

OUR LADY OF GOOD COUNSEL
GENAZZANO, ITALY, 1467

THE TOWN OF GENAZZANO SITS on a hilltop about thirty miles southeast of Rome. There, in 1467, a widow, Petruccia de Geneo, was inspired by the Virgin Mary to rebuild a decrepit church, built in the fifth century and dedicated to Our Lady of Good Counsel. But the widow quickly ran out of funds, and work on the church came to a halt. Instead of helping her or contributing to the project, her neighbors made fun of her and took to calling it "Petruccia's Folly." Still, the widow predicted, "The work will be finished and that right soon, because it is not *my* work, but God's; the Madonna and St. Augustine will do it before I die. Oh, what a noble lady will soon come and take possession of this place."

That same year, on St. Mark's Day (April 25), while the townspeople were gathered in the town square for a celebration, a cloud came down from the sky and enveloped one of the walls of the unfinished church. Then, as untended church bells throughout the town began to ring, the cloud parted and revealed a beautiful portrait of the Virgin Mary and Christ Child. The picture rested on a narrow ledge a few feet off the ground. Petruccia herself proclaimed this to be the "Great Lady" that, as she had prophesied, would take possession of the church.

The people of Genazzano called the painting Madonna de Paradiso on the assumption that angels had brought it from Heaven. But not long afterward,

two men from the Albanian city of Shkodra (Scutari) identified the painting as having come from their city. They had been on their knees praying before it, when it disappeared in a white cloud. At the same time, a mysterious force transported the men through the air to Rome, where their inquiries about the painting soon brought them to Genazzano. It was later determined, or so the legend holds, that the painting flew off the wall of the church in Shkodra the moment the Turks invaded Albania.

A papal commission investigating the painting determined that it had been rendered on a thin layer of plaster of porcelain no thicker than an eggshell. From the moment it appeared in Genazzano, a profusion of miracles were attributed to the painting. Work was soon completed on Petruccia's church and she was buried in the chapel dedicated to the Virgin Mary. During World War II, when Genazzano was in the midst of the war zone, a bomb destroyed the roof of the church, but the painting, recovered from the rubble, was miraculously unharmed. ❧

Johann Eckhard Löffler and Heinrich Löffler, engraving from Flores Seraphici . . . *(detail), Cologne, 1640–1642, Spencer Collection, New York Public Library.*

Nuestra Santísima Madre de la Luz
Guanajuato Province,
Mexico, 1700s

Each year, on July 2, León, a city in the Mexican state of Guanajuato, celebrates the anniversary of the arrival of its miraculous painting of Mary, believed to be the work of her own hand.

In 1850 the painting was credited with saving León from a cholera epidemic, and it supposedly has protected the city from war and revolution on many occasions. In 1876, the keystone of the cathedral's main arch crashed into an aisle during a High Mass. For a moment it looked as if the entire church would collapse on the worshipers, but the bishop placed himself under the arch and prayed to Our Most Holy Mother of the Light, as the Virgin of the painting is known. The cathedral stood.

The painting also has miraculous origins, not in Mexico but in Sicily, where, in the early 1700s, Giovanni Antonio Genovesi, a Jesuit priest known for his devotion to Mary, decided to commission a painting of the Virgin to aid him in his work, which was converting sinners. So he asked a nun to whom the Virgin appeared from time to time to ask Mary how she wanted to be portrayed in the painting.

When the Virgin next appeared to the nun, it was in a blaze of light; she was surrounded by a cortège of angels and held the infant Jesus on one arm. An angel kneeled on one side of her holding up a basket of human hearts, which Jesus blessed by taking them one by one in his hands. With her other hand, the Virgin pulled a sinner away from a monster representing the jaws of Hell.

The nun was so overcome by this vision, which was unlike any she had seen before, that she forgot all about Father Genovesi's painting. But Mary reminded her "of the request you promised to make of me on behalf of one who earnestly appealed to you. I wish the painting to be as you have seen me, and my invocation to be under the title, Most Holy Mother of the Light."

Father Genovesi passed the nun's description of the scene on to an artist in Palermo, but the result was to nobody's liking. Soon Mary appeared again to the nun: "What are you doing here, lazybones, at a time when I need you in Palermo for a matter which concerns my glory." Mary directed the nun to meet her at the artist's studio, where, the Virgin said, the two together

Fernando Aguilár (19th century), Virgin of the Light with Saint Joseph, Saint Michael the Archangel, Saint John Nepomucen, and Saint Anthony/ Virgen de la Luz . . . , Museo Franz Mayer, Mexico City.

LA MADRE S^{ma} DELA LVZ

would help the artist in his task. "When the work is done," the Virgin said, "all shall know by its more than human beauty that a greater mind and a higher art have arranged the composition and laid the colors."

Although the nun was not allowed to leave the convent, she immediately suffered a severe asthma attack, and her doctor sent her at once to Palermo where she would benefit from the climate, and where, of course, both Father Genovesi and the artist resided.

In Palermo, the nun went at once to the artist's studio, where the Virgin appeared to her. As the artist, who could not see the Virgin, began to paint, Mary guided his brush, while the nun gave advice on details and color. The result was, as the Virgin had predicted, a work of "more than human beauty" that only "a greater mind and a higher art" could have created. The Virgin examined the painting, then expressed her pleasure by blessing it with the sign of the cross.

Father Genovesi carried the painting from town to town, leaving behind copies of it when his missionary work in each ended. The painting eventually made its way from Sicily to Mexico, where its travels came to an end in the cathedral in León. Today it is known by its Spanish name, *Nuestra Santísima Madre de la Luz.* ❧

CATHERINE LABOURÉ AND THE MIRACULOUS MEDAL, PARIS, 1830

ON THE NIGHT OF JULY 18, 1830, the eve of the feast of St. Vincent de Paul, a barely literate nun in Paris named Catherine Labouré heard the abbess speak on devotion to the Blessed Virgin. The talk made her so eager to see Mary that before retiring she swallowed a small piece of St. Vincent's surplice, a relic that she had been given earlier, and fell asleep "confident that he would obtain for me the grace of seeing the Blessed Virgin."

At eleven-thirty that same evening she was wakened by a small boy, four or five years old, clothed entirely in white, who called to her, "Sister, Sister, Sister Catherine. Come with me to the chapel; the Blessed Virgin awaits you." Then after being reassured by the child that everyone was fast asleep, Catherine followed him to the chapel where he opened the door with just a light touch of his finger.

There, Catherine recalled, amid a blaze of white light, "I

heard a noise like the rustling of a silk dress," and saw "a lady," her hands radiating beams of light the color of jewels, seated in a chair by the altar steps. When Catherine hesitated, the small boy, whom she came to regard as her guardian angel, assured her that this was the Blessed Virgin. Catherine then fell to her knees and placed her hands in Mary's lap. "There a moment passed, the sweetest of my life," she recalled later in an account precisely titled *July Conversation with the Most Blessed Virgin from 11:30 in the evening of the 18th until 1:30 in the morning of the 19th, St. Vincent's Day.*

During this "conversation," she wrote, the Virgin Mary told her, "My child, the good God wishes to charge you with a mission. You will have much to suffer, but you will rise above these sufferings by reflecting that what you do is for the glory of God. You will know what the good God wants. You will be tormented until you have told him who is charged with directing you. You will be contradicted but, do not fear, you will have grace. Tell with confidence all that passes within you. Tell it with simplicity. Have confidence. Do not be afraid."

Several times during this exchange, the Virgin warned of dire happenings to come: "The times are very evil. Sorrows will befall France; the throne will be overturned. The whole world will be plunged into every kind of misery." When Catherine wondered to herself when this would happen, she wrote, "I understood clearly, *forty years.*" (It is widely believed that Mary had, during this apparition, prophesied the political and social turmoil that occurred in France in 1870, forty years later.)

Catherine's first vision ended when Mary "disappeared like a shadow, as she had come." Catherine then followed the child, who was "resplendent in miraculous light," back to her dormitory, where, she later wrote, "I went back to bed but did not sleep again that night."

Born on May 2, 1806, the ninth of eleven children, Catherine was raised on the family farm in a small village, not far from Dijon, in the Burgundy region of France. At the death of her mother when Catherine was only nine, the distraught child grasped a statue of the Blessed Virgin in her mother's bedroom and said aloud: "Now, dear Blessed Mother, you will be my mother."

The only formal schooling that Catherine ever had was some religious instruction in preparation for her First Communion; after her mother's death much of her youth was spent running

PAGES 142 AND 143: *Elena Climent (b. 1955),* Altar with Photographs and Candles, *1993, Mary-Anne Martin/Fine Art, New York City.*

her father's household. When she was eighteen, Catherine had a dream in which she was frightened by an old priest, whom she was assisting at Mass. "You flee from me now," he called out to her, "but one day you will be glad to come to me. God has plans for you; do not forget it." Later she recognized the old man from a painting she saw as St. Vincent de Paul (1581–1660), founder of the Sisters of Charity. On January 22, 1830, at age twenty-three, Catherine entered that order as a postulant. Three months later she transferred to the seminary at 140 rue du Bac in Paris. There she had a vision of St. Vincent's heart and of Jesus that continued for the nine months of her novitiate and, some of her chroniclers suspect, for the rest of her life.

Catherine's second vision of Mary, about five-thirty on the evening of November 27, 1830, was preceded by the same sound of "the rustling of a silk dress, from the tribune near the picture of St. Joseph." Then the Virgin, dressed entirely in white, appeared. "A white veil covered her head and fell on either side to her feet. Under the veil her hair, in coils, was bound with a fillet ornamented with lace, about three centimeters in height or of two fingers' breadth, without pleats, and resting lightly on the hair. Her face was sufficiently exposed, indeed exposed very well, and so beautiful that it seems to me impossible to express her ravishing beauty."

In this vision, Mary held a golden ball topped with a little golden cross; the ball, a voice told Catherine, represented "the whole world, especially France, and each person in particular." On each of her fingers she wore three rings from which rays of light flashed. The Virgin stood on a white globe. A serpent, "green in color with yellow spots," completed the picture.

As Catherine watched, a frame "slightly oval in shape, formed round the Blessed Virgin. Within it was written in letters of gold: 'O Mary, conceived without sin, pray for us who have recourse to thee.'"

Then the same voice explained her mission: "'Have a medal struck after this model. All who wear it will receive great graces; they should wear it around the neck. Graces will abound for those who wear it with confidence.'" As the voice faded out, the tableau turned, revealing on the reverse side "a large M surmounted by a bar and a cross; beneath the M were the Hearts of Jesus and Mary, the one crowned with thorns, the other pierced with a sword."

When Catherine told her confessor, a young priest named

Aladel, of the visions and the Virgin's desire for a medal, he was skeptical, seeing "nothing in it but the work of her imagination." The response to his indifference, the Virgin assured Catherine, was patience, for, "When the time comes, he will do as I wish, for he is my servant, and he would not wish to displease me." Catherine's persistence—and the fear that he might be incurring the Virgin's displeasure by his indifference—finally induced M. Aladel to obtain permission from the Archbishop of Paris to have the medal struck. (French priests who did not belong to orders were called Monsieur, not Father.) The archbishop saw in the story of the apparition nothing "at variance with the faith of the Church and the devotion of the faithful." In fact, he asked that the first medal be given to him.

Fifteen hundred copies of the Medal of the Immaculate Conception, as it was first called, were minted in June 1832. Success was immediate; by 1836 more than two million medals had been produced. Soon a variety of miracles were being attributed to it, hence the name by which it is known today, the Miraculous Medal. An account written by M. Aladel of its miraculous works includes cures of "insanity, leprosy, scurvy, tuberculosis, tumors, dropsy, epilepsy, hernia, paralysis, typhoid and other fevers, canker, fractures, scrofula, palpitation of the heart and cholera." In the same account, the priest gave the medal credit for "the conversion of hardened sinners, of Protestants, of Jews, of apostates, of unbelievers, of Freemasons, of evildoers and persons of light character," and attributed to it "protection and preservation in war, in shipwreck, in accidents, and in duels."

Catherine Labouré went on to live a life of obscurity with only her confessor knowing her connection with the medal. For forty-six years she took care of the elderly and tended the chicken coop at the Sisters of Charity residence outside Paris, where she was described as "matter-of-fact, unexcitable, insignificant, cold, and apathetic." She also suffered periods of temporary amnesia, so she was able to plead a memory lapse in 1836 when Church authorities wanted her to testify at an official inquiry into the medal's origins.

Catherine died on December 31, 1876. She was beatified in 1933 and canonized in 1947. She is buried in the convent chapel at 140 rue du Bac, the place where the Blessed Virgin Mary first appeared to her. Since her visions, untold millions of the Miraculous Medal have been distributed throughout the world. ❧

Lady of Legend

B Y THE ELEVENTH CENTURY, devotion to Mary was widespread, with "her miracles on every lip," as one historian has put it. These miracles, more legend than fact, were not grounded in any specific person, place, or time. (Frequently they begin vaguely: "A certain young knight in the flower of his youth . . ." "A certain cloistered nun . . . ," etc.) In the Middle Ages, these tales were the plots of plays, the subject of sermons, and the essence of folk tales. Usually they celebrate Mary's encompassing love for mankind, especially sinners, and her influence with her Son, who, as He Himself admits in many legends, can deny His mother nothing. The stories also elicit the comforting thought (or is it a warning?) that nobody who loves Mary will be denied salvation.

These lusty tales are imaginative in their presentation of human failing—and in the lengths Mary will go to redeem the fallen. Women (often nuns) in trouble with men are regularly rescued by Mary. So are wellborn youths who have gone astray, usually squandering fortunes in the process. Mary restores severed body parts, brings sinners back to life—so they can repent—cures the sick, preserves chastity, and saves the endangered. The stories end happily, with everybody involved praising and serving "our holy Lady, the Virgin twofold, Mary, all the days of their lives."

Nahum B. Zenil (b. 1947), Blessings/Benediciones, *1990,*
Collection of Sra. Yolanda Santos de Garza Lagüera, Monterrey, Mexico.

MARY AND THE ONE-EYED CLERK

A CLERK IN PARIS WHO WAS devoted to the Virgin Mary wanted nothing more in life than to see her in all her beauty. His prayers were answered when an angel came to him with word from Mary that "on such a day and hour" she would appear to him. But, the angel warned him, after he had seen the Virgin, he would become blind. And the clerk replied: "I will gladly lose my sight to deserve to see her once."

After the angel left, the clerk began to have second thoughts. How would he live without his sight? "I will not be able to earn my bread and will certainly become a wretched beggar." Then a solution occurred to him: when Mary appeared he would open only one eye, "and thus I shall lose one eye and, if one remains to me, it will be enough."

So when the Virgin appeared he covered one eye with his hand and with the other "looked upon such beauty and splendor as cannot be expressed in words conceived in the heart." After the Virgin disappeared, the clerk could still see with one eye, but he nonetheless reproached himself: "Why did I close one eye, wretched man, and not open both. Gladly would I be blind if I might see her more fully."

The one-eyed clerk prayed to see Mary again, and, after a long time, the angel appeared again, saying that he would see Mary one more time "inasmuch as you wish to lose the other eye." But when Mary appeared, this did not happen. Instead, the sight in the other was restored, and the clerk could see Mary in all her beauty and glory with both eyes.

This account of the miracle of the clerk concludes with a passage from St. Anselm's *Meditations:* "Mary, thou art beautiful to gaze upon, desirable to embrace, delightful to see, for the greatest joy next to God is to look on thee and to take delight in thy praises." ✢

ZACHARIAH AND THE FIFTY ROSES

ZACHARIAH WAS A NOBLE AND handsome youth whose "heart burned as with fire by reason of the ardor of his love for our holy Lady, the Virgin Mary." To honor her with a gift, he vowed to pre-sent her, every day, with a crown of fifty roses, which he made himself and fastened to a picture of her in a church. When the season for the roses was over, he vowed to "give unto thee fifty salutations instead of the fifty roses."

One day, after he had become a man, he was traveling along a strange road, when he remembered that he had not recited the fifty salutations that day. So he left the road and went into the wilderness to be alone in his devotions. A captain of thieves, who intended to rob Zachariah, was watching him from a hiding place, when he saw "a lady come down from heaven with great glory, and there were beautiful virgins with her." And as Zachariah prayed—and the captain looked on in astonishment—roses began to drop out of Zachariah's mouth with every word he uttered. The Virgin gathered up the roses, until she had fifty of them; then she blessed Zachariah and went back to heaven.

When Zachariah rose from his knees to resume his journey, the captain of the thieves seized him and asked him about the beautiful women that he had seen descending from heaven. Since Zachariah had not seen the vision, he could tell the thief nothing, but he did explain how he offered fifty salutations to the Virgin Mary each day. The captain of the thieves then realized he had witnessed a miracle and vowed to repent and to serve "the Lady of us all, the holy woman, the Virgin twofold, Mary, all the days of my life." After the captain told his band of thieves what he had seen, they released Zachariah and allowed him to continue, unharmed, on his way. Then the thieves, too, repented and became monks, "and they served our holy Lady, the Virgin twofold, Mary, all the days of their lives." ⚬

MARY AND THE PREGNANT ABBESS

BECAUSE SHE WAS BEAUTIFUL AND God-fearing—and "loved our Holy Lady, the Virgin Mary, with her whole heart"—an abbess in charge of a nunnery was hated by the devil and resented by her nuns, whom "she governed strictly." To bring about her downfall, the devil instilled evil and lustful thoughts in her and soon, "through his secret prompting," she became pregnant by her page. Although she tried to conceal this fact from the other nuns, she could not, and they gleefully sent word to the bishop that she was with child.

When the abbess learned that the bishop was on his way to the nunnery, she knew that she had been betrayed and went in despair to the chapel,

where she prayed to Mary: "O thou who lovest mercy and compassion, make soft thy heart toward thy sinful handmaiden who hath been entrapped in a snare, and show loving kindness unto her, and do away the wickedness which I bear in my womb . . ."

That night the Virgin Mary came to the abbess in a dream and told her, "I have made supplication to my Son to forgive thee thy sin, but thou must never commit the sin again." Then Mary sent two angels to take the child from her womb and to give it to a hermit who lived nearby. When the abbess awoke, she knew that she was no longer pregnant. But she still had to face the bishop, and when he asked her about reports that she had "become with child by fornication," she denied it. And when further examination proved that she was not pregnant, the bishop apologized profusely and then began to chastise the nuns who had accused her.

The abbess now feared that the bishop might expel the nuns from the convent, so she confessed her sin to him and told him about the Virgin's intervention, and he "marveled exceedingly" at this evidence that a miracle had occurred. He then sent for the child and raised him in his own house and taught him the Psalms of David and the stories of the saints, so that "the Holy Spirit came upon him in abundance, and the love of our Holy Lady, the Virgin Mary, was with him in full measure." When the bishop died, the young man, the abbess's grown son, became bishop in his stead. ⌀

THE VIRGIN GIVES A HAND

Piero della Francesca (1410/20–1492), Madonna del Parto, *Chapel of the Cemetery, Monterchi.*

THERE ONCE WAS A BISHOP, A GOOD and holy man, who feared God and "kept himself from unchastity and from meditation upon evil." At the time he lived, it was the custom for communicants about to receive the Eucharist to embrace the hands and feet of the priest. One day, as he was consecrating the host, a woman took hold of his hands and "the unclean desire of the flesh entered into his heart, and he burned with the flame of lust."

When the service was finished, the bishop went into the room where the church's treasures were stored and, with a sharp knife, cut off the offending hand. He stayed there weeping, and when the other priests found him they led him to a picture of the Virgin Mary where he "entreated her to have mercy upon him and to help him and to pardon his sin." No sooner had he said this than the Virgin Mary appeared to him. She took his severed hand in her hands and reattached it to his arm, so that "no mark whatsoever of the cut could be found." Then, as the priests and the deacons marveled at this miracle, she disappeared. ❧

MARY TO THE RESCUE

THERE WAS A POOR MAN WHO supported himself and his wife by going, at the end of the day, into a gold mine in a high mountain and collecting tiny flecks of the precious metal that the miners could not be bothered with. As proof of his and his wife's devotion to Mary, the man gave the church, each day, one loaf of bread, one vessel of wine, one wax candle, and two dirhams of incense. As he did this, he would say, "I come to thy house . . . and I give offerings according to my ability."

One day, while the poor man was inside the mine, it collapsed, and the entrance was blocked with earth and stone. When the miners saw this the next day, they cried out, "Behold, the poor man is dead and is buried in the gallery of the mine." And his wife, when she learned of his death, prayed to Mary: "O thou boast of all the world, Queen of Women, Mother of the Redeemer, behold, my lord is buried deep in the mine and I have not got his body to

bury in thy church." She asked Mary to intercede and promised to continue his daily gift of one loaf, one vessel of wine, one candle, and two dirhams of incense.

The grieving wife did this for twelve days; but each time she presented the gift to the gatekeeper of the church, the offerings mysteriously disappeared as soon as his back was turned. In the meantime, the men of the town were digging out the collapsed mine, and on the twelfth day they finally came to the place where the poor man was entombed. But instead of finding a corpse, they found him in perfect health. "How hast thou continued to exist in the belly of the earth all the past twelve days?" they asked.

The man explained to his rescuers that, when the mine collapsed, two pillars, one on either side of him, suddenly appeared to support the earth above his head, "and I have remained here until this present in safety, comfort, and rest, and no harm of any kind has befallen me; on the contrary, I seem to have been in a beautiful house."

When they asked him what he ate during that time, the poor man explained that the Virgin Mary brought him, each day, one loaf of bread, one vessel of wine, one wax candle, and two dirhams of incense. And she said to him: "This loaf of bread shall serve as your food, and this vessel of wine shall be for the joy of your heart, and this wax candle shall burn before you by day and by night so that the darkness may not overwhelm you, and this incense shall serve you for sweet perfume."

After his sojourn in the mine was over, the poor man was rejoined with his loving wife, but soon thereafter they both forsook the world. He became a monk and she a nun, and, this story concludes, "They both continued to serve and worship our Lady Mary with a pure heart and a good mind until they departed from this world." ❧

GUARDIAN OF ALL CHASTITY

HAVING LISTENED TO THE EVIL promptings of the devil, the wife of a knight committed adultery with another soldier. Eventually she repented and, while grieving for her sin, refused to have anything more to do with her former lover.

He, however, still desired her and one night, when her husband was away, he entered her house and tried to tempt her. At first she refused, but, when he began to force her, she called on "the guardian of all chastity," crying out: "I beg thee, Lady, by the sacred 'Hail Mary,' to deliver me."

The words had the desired effect; according to an account written at the time, all the spirit went out of the soldier and he withered, "and so the woman escaped unhurt." As for the soldier, who now knew what Mary could and would do, he never dared say another word to tempt the woman or anyone else. ❧

SINFUL BUT CHASTE

A NOBLE YOUTH, WHO HAD squandered his entire inheritance "on dicing and taverns," had one redeeming feature: through all the debauchery, amid myriad temptations, he had kept himself chaste.

The foolish youth, who was now homeless and wandering wretchedly about his native land, had a pious uncle who took pity on him. "Could you bring yourself to do one thing for me?" the uncle asked. When his nephew agreed, the uncle said: "I want you every day to salute the glorious Mary, Mother of God, fifty times." And the youth answered sadly that he would try to honor his uncle's request. "I wish that I could salute her just once, let alone fifty times," he said.

A year passed. The uncle met his nephew again and asked him if he had kept his promise. And when the youth replied that he had—and that saluting Mary "comes before my worldly affairs"—the uncle rejoiced, then asked his nephew to double the number of salutations to one hundred a day. And the youth agreed to this request as well.

At the end of the second year, the young man reported to his uncle: "Through the intercessions of the Mother of Christ all the madness and misery of my condition has vanished and all the strength of my will is fixed in a firm resolve to do right." So the uncle asked the nephew to increase the salutations to one hundred and fifty ("thrice fifty salutations") and promised, if he did this, to find him a suitable bride at the end of the year. "The youth agreed," the story reads, and, in his determination to honor the Virgin Mary, he "proved steadfast."

So the uncle, honoring his commitment, arranged a marriage for his nephew. The wedding day promised to be a happy occasion; at a banquet after the ceremony, the bride and groom and all their relatives were seated around a table celebrating the marriage, when the youth remembered that he had neglected his daily salutations, so he excused himself from the feast and left the room to pray. As he was completing his salutations, the Virgin Mary appeared to him and said: "Behold, your salutations have been written in gold, because, despite your trifling and waywardness, you did keep your body in clean chastity. Soon a deadly fever shall seize you, and on the third day you shall come to me without any stain on your flesh."

Greatly subdued, the youth returned to the celebration and told his relatives to continue the feast without him. He had lost his appetite, he said, and was going to retire to his room. There he gathered his closest friends around his bed and told them that Mary had appeared during his prayers and had told him that his life would soon be over.

On the third day, just as Mary had foretold, the youth died. "But, his bride," the story concludes, "being unwilling to marry anyone else, afterwards remained a pure virgin." ✀

English or French School (?), The Wilton Diptych (detail, right-hand panel), c. 1395, The National Gallery, London.

A Gift of Words

A servant of a parish priest, a man who had been deaf and mute all his life, fell deathly ill, and, as he lay on his bed awaiting the end, the Virgin Mary came to him and gave him speech and hearing. Then she commanded: "Get a priest to come to you—repent and confess your sins, take the sacrament of the Body of Our Lord Jesus Christ, my Son, and afterward I will carry you to the rest prepared for you."

The deaf mute called for the priest, his master—much to the amazement of those gathered around his bed, because they had never heard him talk—and received the sacrament. Afterward they asked him how it was that he could talk and hear and he told them about the visit of the Virgin. Had he ever done her any special service? they wanted to know, and he replied that there was none that he knew about. However, he had seen the priest fasting on Saturday, and, since he had assumed that the priest had pious reasons for doing so, he had fasted too.

The parish priest then confirmed that his faithful servant was indeed telling the truth: "He has always fasted on the Saturday, when I was in the habit of fasting in honor of the Blessed Virgin Mary."

Hearing this, the account of the miracle goes, those in the dying man's presence "praised God and the glorious Blessed Virgin Mary, his mother, with great amazement and joyful voice, since she had not abandoned those who had faith in her and those who served her." ⁓

The Cannibal Redeemed

"Now there was a certain man in the city of Kemer, and he was of noble race and was, in name, a Christian, but his sin was very great, and indeed it exceeded that of all other men, for he did not eat ordinary food and the flesh of oxen, but he lived upon human flesh."

So begins the story of the Virgin Mary and the Cannibal.

This man with a taste for humans was, in fact, in a dilemma, for he was running out of victims, having eaten practically everybody near him, some seventy-eight people, including friends, relatives, servants, and—but only as a last resort—his wife and two children.

So, to search out his next meal, the cannibal took to the

road. There he encountered a leper covered with sores. "He wanted to eat the poor man," the account goes, "but he did not like him because of his sores which were putrefying and which stank exceedingly." The beggar was dying of thirst and begged the cannibal—in the name of God—to give him some water, and the man refused. Then the beggar asked again—for the sake of heaven and earth—and again the cannibal said no. Finally the beggar asked: "In the name of Mary, give me water to drink before my soul shall depart." This moved the man, who replied: "Take and drink, for Mary's sake."

When the cannibal died and the angels of darkness claimed his soul, Mary went to her Son on the man's behalf, asking for compassion. "What has he done for thee?" the Son asked His mother. And when she told Him how the cannibal had given water in her name to the beggar, Jesus ordered the angels, "Bring forth the scales and weigh the souls that he hath devoured against the water that he gave the thirsty man to drink." And when they did this, it turned out that the few drops of water outweighed all the seventy-eight souls. This outcome caused the angels to marvel "and they gave shouts of joy because the cannibal was saved and was made to live through the entreaty of our holy Lady Mary, the twofold Virgin, the God-bearer, through whom all things come to pass." ❧

MARY AND A MOTHER'S SHAME

A MAN AND WIFE, RICH BUT CHILD-less, prayed to the martyrs, saints, and the Virgin Mary for a child. God heard their prayers and, to their great joy, gave them a man child. The father loved the child so much that he saved all his money for him and stopped giving alms to the poor and doing other acts of kindness as he had before. Finally he said to himself, "Woe is me! Because of this boy, I have ceased to do good. It is best for me to forsake the world and all that therein is and to go and save my soul." So he left his family and entered a monastery.

The mother also loved the boy to excess. According to the story, she made him sleep in her bed even after he had become a man and had "learned to know women carnally." One night, "Satan set the shameful thing between them, and seduced them, and at length the son committed fornication with his

Durch die Anrufung Maria ist geholfen worden. 1882

mother and she conceived."

The mother was afraid that her neighbors would discover her sin, so she increased her giving to the poor and the church and "served our Lady Mary and looked to her to protect her." And when the baby was born, "she cast it away."

Satan, however, knew every detail of what had happened, and, disguising himself as a wise man, he told the king, who summoned the woman. When she came before the king, he said to Satan, "Here is the woman." But Satan was afraid, because he could see another woman beside her, who was Mary, whose face he could not look upon. And, as all people of the city gathered together, the Virgin Mary began to speak with joy and gladness. And when Satan heard her words, "he melted away like smoke." So the king forgave the shameful woman and the story happily concludes: "Thereupon the people knew that the affair was the work of Satan and that it was caused by his jealousy of the deeds which the woman had been wont to do. And all this took place through the petition of our Lady Mary." ⅏

MARY GIVES BACK ALL

A YOUNG MAN WHO HAD INHERITed great wealth was forced by financial difficulties to sell most of his property to a knight. This made him exceedingly sad, and when his steward asked him, "Do you wish to be rich?" the youth replied, "If I may have riches with God's will."

So the steward led him to the devil. To the steward's request that he restore the youth's riches, the devil said: "If he is willing to be devoted to me, I will give him riches beyond all his kinsmen and neighbors." When the young man pledged that he would be faithful and obedient, the devil explained that the man must also renounce "the Highest." This caused the youth to hesitate, but, urged on by his steward, he did deny God.

But that was not all. "Your task is still unfinished," the devil said. "You must also renounce the Mother of the Highest, for she is the one that causes us the greatest loss. Those whom the Son condemns by righteous judgment, she brings to Him in mercy and forgiveness."

This demand troubled and frightened the young man. "You have already done what is worse," the steward reasoned. "Do now what is less. You have denied your Creator. Deny now

Lower Bavaria (Pilgramsberg), 19th century, In Gratitude to the Virgin, *1882, Bavarian National Museum, Munich.*

the creature too." But the young man refused: "I will never deny her even if I have to remain a beggar forever."

So the young man and the steward left the devil, the deal unconsummated, and on their way back they passed a church which the youth entered. There, before an image of the Virgin Mary holding her Child in her arms, he began to pray, filling the church with his cries and moans. At the same time, the knight to whom he had sold his property entered the church, and, seeing the young man imploring the Virgin, he stepped behind a pillar to see what would happen.

As the knight and the steward looked on, the Virgin in the image turned to the Son in her arms and said, "Sweetest Son, pity this man." But the Child only turned his face away. Then the Virgin placed her Son on the altar and prostrated herself before Him, saying, "I beg you, my Son, for my sake to remit his sins." Immediately the Infant replied: "Mother, I could never deny thee anything. Behold for thy sake I wholly remit his sin." And the young man left the church, still sad at what he had done, but glad that he had been forgiven.

Outside, the knight, who had witnessed the entire scene, stopped the youth. "Sir," he said, "I am not ignorant of the cause of your sadness." Then he offered the young man the hand of his only daughter in marriage. And, as her dowry, he added, "I will give you back all your goods, and I will besides make you heir to my own wealth."

So the young man was married and faithfully served the Blessed Virgin Mary for the rest of his life, for, as the story was originally told, "through her he obtained remission of his sins and, moreover, the comfort of worldly possessions." ⚬

By the Dew of Her Milk

A CLERIC, WHO DEVOTEDLY SALUTed the Virgin Mary each day, praising also her "blessed womb, which carried Thee, O Christ, and paps that gave suck to our Lord and Saviour," was taken ill. His sickness caused him such agony "that he bit through his tongue and lips, and would have done the same to his limbs had he not been prevented."

As he lay in his sickbed near death, he suddenly cried out: "O Lady of Mercy, Fount of Pity, is this the reward given to the faithful? Is this the tongue so wont in ardent love and by long custom to salute thy body, thy breasts

and childbirth, so that hardly aught else could ever be heard in the church of God? Let not the hopes of men come to naught by finding first in thee no refuge."

At these imploring words, the Virgin Mary suddenly appeared in his room and drew near his bed. Then, "as if to make amends for the neglect of her servant with which she was charged," she drew out one of her breasts and put it into the mouth of the sick man. And "as the dew of her sacred milk was poured into it," his tongue and lips were miraculously restored and he arose from his bed, in perfect health. From then on he gave himself completely to the service of God and "lived a religious and godly man to the end of his life." ❧

Peruvian, late 18th century, Cuzco School, Nursing Madonna, *New Orleans Museum of Art.*

Mary's Warnings

BEGINNING IN THE NINETEENTH CENTURY, the Virgin, in many of her appearances, cautioned mankind to mend its errant ways or face the wrath of an angry God. Her power to "restrain" the arm of her Son might soon fail her, she tells those who see or hear her.

In the twentieth century, the ominous messages became stronger, more explicit, and more relevant to world events. Although Mary's words at Fátima, Portugal, in 1917, were somewhat cryptic, many Catholics believe she accurately predicted World War II and the spread of communism. At Garabandal, Spain, in the 1960s, Mary at times was playful, but the heart of her message was apocalyptic, with references to "the cup filling up" or "brimming over" and, for the seers, visions of a punishment that was, in Conchita González's words, "more dreadful than anything we can imagine."

In a series of continuing apparitions and locutions that began in 1970, Mary has described, through a seer in Bayside, Queens, New York, a deadly "Ball of Redemption" heading toward earth. In Akita, Japan, in 1973, a statue of Mary warned a deaf nun that humanity faces a punishment more terrible than the Flood, but she tempered the message with assurances that those who believe in her will be spared. Akita is one of the few modern apparitions approved by the Catholic Church.

Odilon Redon (1840–1916), Virgin of the Dawn, *1890, Collection of Mr. and Mrs. Robert Donnelley.*

WHERE THE SUN DANCED
FÁTIMA, PORTUGAL, 1917

THE APPARITIONS AT FÁTIMA, Portugal, in 1917 started reassuringly enough, with the Virgin Mary, dressed in resplendent white, floating in over the treetops and urging the three children to whom she appeared to pray and say the rosary. However, on the third of her appearances, which came a month apart, she revealed that the visions at Fátima had a more ominous purpose: to warn mankind of God's threatened punishment. As the children looked on in terror, the Virgin showed them a vision of Hell, which was, in Lucia Abóbora's words, "a sea of fire; and plunged in this fire the demons and the souls, as if they were red-hot coals, . . . among shrieks and groans of sorrow and despair which horrify and cause to shudder with fear."

When the children could stand the sight of the inferno no longer, they looked away, raising their eyes to the Virgin, who was looking down on them tenderly. She then said: "You see Hell, where the souls of poor sinners go. To save them God wishes to establish in the world the devotion to my Immaculate Heart. If they do what I will tell you, many souls will be saved, and there will be peace. The war

is going to end. But if they do not stop offending God another and worse one will begin in the reign of Pius XI." With these words, many believe, Mary foretold the end of World War I and, since Pius XI was Pope from 1922 to 1939, the beginning of World War II.

The apparitions at Fátima began on May 13, 1917, as ten-year-old Lucia Abóbora and her younger cousins, Jacinta and Francisco Martos, were tending sheep in a vale known as the Cova da Iria. When a storm blew up, they ran for shelter and then they saw, hovering over the branches of an oak tree, "a Lady dressed all in white, more brilliant than the sun, shedding rays of light clearer and stronger than a crystal glass filled with the most sparkling water and pierced by the burning rays of the sun." She was young, indescribably beautiful, and dressed in a gleaming white robe that was adorned with a star near the hem at her feet. In her hands, which were crossed on her breast, she held a white rosary on a chain of white pearls.

To Lucia's question, "Where do you come from?" the Lady replied that she came from Heaven. She explained that she wanted the children to return to that same place on the thirteenth day every month for five months: "In the month of October I will tell you who I am and what I want you to do." Lucia asked if she and Jacinta and Francisco would go to Heaven and the Lady replied that they would, except that Francisco "will first have to say many rosaries." When Lucia asked about two young woman in the village who had died recently, she was informed that one was in Heaven, and that the other would be in Purgatory until "the end of the world."

Before she departed by melding into the sunlight, the Lady told the children, "You will suffer much, but God's grace will strengthen you. My children, go on saying the rosary just as you have done."

Although this was the first of six apparitions of the Blessed Virgin Mary, as the Lady would later identify herself, it was not the first vision that the young seers had experienced; in 1915, Lucia and her two cousins observed a white cloud-like form hovering near them as they tended sheep. The next year Lucia, now nine, and her two cousins, Jacinta, six, and Francisco, eight, had three visits from a young man of dazzling whiteness who called himself the Angel of Peace. But

it was Mary's appearances in 1917 that attracted the attention of the world and transformed Fátima from a rural village into one of the most important shrines in Europe.

As word of the 1917 apparition spread through the town, the children became subjects of scorn and ridicule. Still, some sixty people were in the Cova da Iria on the thirteenth of the next month.

JUNE 13, 1917: As they waited in the shade of a large oak tree, Lucia quieted the others and cried: "Our Lady is coming!" When she appeared, invisible to all except the three children, she told them to say their rosary but to add after each decade these words: "Oh, my Jesus, forgive us our sins. Save us from the fire of Hell and lead all souls to Heaven, especially those who have the most need of Thy Mercy."

The Lady also told Lucia to learn to read and write (all three children were illiterate), adding that "I will come soon and take Francisco and Jacinta. But you are to stay here a longer time. God wishes to use you to make me known and loved, to establish throughout the world devotion to my Immaculate Heart. To all those who embrace it I promise salvation, and their souls will be loved by God as flowers placed by me before His throne." The prospect of being left alone without her companions upset Lucia, but the Lady reassured her: "I will never leave you . . . remember that my Immaculate Heart will ever be your refuge and the way that will lead you to God." Then the Lady extended her hands and rays of light shone from them. In her right hand was a heart pierced with thorns. As she rose and began to disappear, people in the crowd saw a white cloud rising slowly and some of the branches on the oak tree appeared to bend toward the east.

In the month that followed, pressure was put on the children to deny their visions, and they were told that the apparitions were the work of the devil. Lucia, who was plagued with doubt, even considered staying home on July 13. But when the day came, she joined Jacinta and Francisco at the Cova da Iria, where some five thousand people had gathered.

July 13: When the Lady appeared, Lucia asked her for "a miracle so that all the people will know that you really do appear to us," and the figure answered that, in October, she would not only reveal her identity, as already promised, but also "work a miracle so great that all will believe in the reality of the apparitions."

It was also at this third apparition that she imparted three "secrets" to the children. The first was the vision of Hell, after which she spoke of a sign— "a night illuminated by an unknown light"—that will mean that God "is going to punish the world for its crimes by means of war, hunger, and persecution of the Church and of the Holy Father."

The second secret was both a request and a prophecy. She said:

To prevent this I come to ask the consecration of Russia to my Immaculate Heart and the Communion of reparation on the first Saturdays. If they listen to my requests, Russia will be converted and there will be peace. If not, she will spread her errors through the entire world, provoking wars and persecutions of the Church. The good will be martyrized, the Holy Father will have much to suffer, various nations will be annihilated.

In the end my Immaculate Heart will triumph. The Holy Father will consecrate Russia to me, and it will be converted and a certain period of peace will be granted to humanity.

The third secret has never been revealed.

August 13: While some eighteen thousand people waited at the Cova da Iria, the children were in the custody of the local administrator, an anticlerical fanatic named Arturo de Oliveira

Geertgen tot Sint Jans (1455/65–1485/95), The Glorification of the Virgin, Museum Boymans-van Beuningen, Rotterdam.

Santos, who detained them in a desperate attempt to frighten them into renouncing their story or revealing the contents of the secrets. When even his threat to fry them in oil did not bring forth a confession, he returned them home on August 16.

August 19: As the children were tending their sheep at a place known as Valinhos, the Lady unexpectedly appeared. She was displeased that the children had not come as expected on August 13, and said that the actions of the administrator would make the miracle promised for October 13 less impressive than originally promised. The children brought home a tree branch which the Lady's foot had touched, and when Lucia's mother examined it closely, a sweet odor emanated from it.

September 13: Many in the immense crowd awaiting the fifth apparition at Cova da Iria believed they saw the sun dim and a luminous globe appear in the sky at the same time the children saw the Lady. At this apparition she told the children that both the Christ Child and St. Joseph would be with her when she appeared in a month. Lucia asked her to cure the sick and the Lady answered: "I will cure some of them but not all, because the Lord has no confidence in them."

By now all of Portugal and much of Europe knew about the apparitions at Fátima and about the promised miracle of October 13. On that day some seventy thousand people, many of them drenched from a terrible storm on the night of October 12, had crowded into the village. The throngs made Lucia's mother nervous; if a miracle did not take place, she was afraid that they would take out their disappointment on the family.

October 13: The final appearance of the Lady was brief. "What do you want of me?" Lucia asked, her face radiant with ecstasy. The Lady replied, "I want you to have them build a chapel here in my honor. I am the Lady of the Rosary. Let them continue to say the rosary every day. The war is going to end, and the soldiers will soon return to their homes." When Lucia asked about the curing of the sick and the conversion of sinners, the Lady said, "Some yes, others no . . . ," adding, "let them offend Our Lord God no more, for He is already much offended."

The Lady, whom Lucia now knew to be the Virgin Mary, then disappeared in a blaze of radiant light. Next, a tableau of the Holy Family appeared to the children: St. Joseph with the Christ Child on his arm, Mary dressed in traditional white with a blue mantle. After Lucia said aloud, so the crowd could hear her, "Saint Joseph is going to bless us," all three children saw Joseph and the Child make the sign of the cross over the crowd three times. But only Lucia saw the next two tableaux: the Virgin Mary in somber dress as Our Lady of Sorrows with a sorrowful Christ by her side, and, lastly, Mary, appearing as Our Lady of Mount Carmel with her infant Son on her knee, crowned as the Queen of Heaven and the Queen of the World.

At this point, Lucia cried, "Look at the sun!" although she later could not recall uttering those words. The sequence that followed was taken by many who saw it as the miracle that the Virgin Mary had promised for October 13. First, the sun began to "dance" and whirl and tremble, then plunge in a zigzag course toward the earth, before resuming its original place in the sky. This display, which many witnesses feared signaled the end of the world, was described by one witness: "The great star of day makes one think of a silver plaque, and it is possible to look straight at it without the least discomfort. It does not burn, it does not blind. . . . But now bursts forth a colossal clamor, and we hear the nearest spectators crying, 'Miracle, miracle! Marvel, marvel.'"

In the aftermath of the apparitions at Fátima, the Virgin's prophecy about the fate of the children came true. Francisco died of influenza a year and a half later, on April 4, 1918, the day after he received his First Communion. Jacinta also fell victim to the epidemic and died on February 20, 1920. After their deaths, life became even more difficult for Lucia, who had been the object of much curiosity and scrutiny ever since the apparitions. In 1922 she entered a boarding school run by the Sisters of St. Dorothy and, in 1926, she joined the order's novitiate. She stayed with the Sisters of St. Dorothy until 1948, when she became a Carmelite sister.

There is still considerable confusion about the disposition of the third secret of Fátima. Lucia, when she was seriously ill, wrote down the contents of the secret, probably in early 1944, and sealed it in an envelope with instructions that it was not to be opened until 1960. The envelope remained in the possession of the Bishop of Leira, Portugal (who posed with it for *Life* Magazine in 1948), until 1957 when he sent it to the Vatican. It is widely supposed that Pope John XXIII opened the letter in 1960, but its contents have never been revealed. ❧

A Call to
Penance and Sacrifice
Garabandal, Spain, 1961–1965

Just after they had stolen some apples from a tree on Sunday evening, June 18, 1961, four young girls in a village in Spain called San Sebastián de Garabandal were startled by a loud clap of thunder. They took this to be a sign, in the words of Conchita González, then twelve years old, that the theft had "made the devil happy and our guardian angels sad." To fend off the devil, they began throwing stones to their left, the side on which they believed the devil resided.

Suddenly "a most beautiful figure with a great deal of light" appeared to them. Although they were very frightened, the girls could see that it was a beautiful angel, strong in build but with the face of a boy of about nine. He wore a blue tunic and he had dark eyes and tan skin. His wings were large but not attached to his body. "They were more like a halo would be, like a light gleaming from behind him."

The girls ran to the village church, where they began to tell the rest of the village about the apparition. The next day they returned to the grove of pines where they had seen the vision, but the angel did not appear.

That night, while she was praying, Conchita heard a reassuring voice: "Don't worry. You shall see me again." The following Wednesday, the angel made the first of eight more appearances. During one of these visions, the girls saw writing beneath the angel, but paid little attention to it; on July 1 the angel told them that the Virgin Mary, "under the title of Our Lady of Mount Carmel," would appear to them the next day.

The girls returned to the same spot on Sunday, July 2, when, as promised, the Virgin Mary appeared with an angel on each side of her. One of them they recognized as the angel who had appeared to them previously; they would later learn he was St. Michael the Archangel. Next to one of the angels was a large eye which they assumed was the eye of God. To the girls, Mary appeared to be about eighteen years old. She wore a white dress, a blue mantle, and a crown of golden starlets. A chestnut-colored scapular hung from her right wrist. "Her mouth is delicate and very beautiful, very unusual. I do not know how to explain it. There is no woman that resembles the

Giambattista Tiepolo (1696–1770), The Immaculate Conception, (detail),1769, Museo del Prado.

Virgin in voice, appearance, or anything," Conchita said.

Conchita and her companions, María Dolores, Jacinta, and María Cruz, saw the Virgin more than two thousand times between 1961 and 1965. As the apparitions continued, the Virgin appeared to them almost anywhere, often at a clump of pine trees just outside the village, but at many other places in and around the village. At first Mary appeared to the girls only when they were together; later, the apparitions often occurred to them individually when they were apart.

On July 4, 1961, the Virgin asked the children if they understood some words that had appeared under the archangel in June. When they said they had not, the Virgin passed on this message for them to announce publicly the following October 18:

*T*here must be many sacrifices, much penance. We must visit the Blessed Sacrament frequently. But, first, we must lead good lives. If we do not, we will be punished. The cup is already filling up and, if we do not change, the punishment will be very great.

On two nights in June the following year, Conchita and two of the others had a terrifying experience in which they were shown a vision of the punishment the Virgin warned about. Later Conchita said: "I cannot state the nature of the punishment, . . . except that it will be the result of a direct intervention from God which is more dreadful than anything we can imagine."

Most of the Virgin's appearances at Garabandal were more mundane and more joyful. Conchita recounted how Mary "played with us and kissed us. People who saw us said that we would laugh with our whole bodies." In their accounts, the children stressed that the Virgin was life-like in appearance and action—"like you or me here, very natural, just extremely beautiful and graceful." During the first apparition, for instance, "we talked much with the Virgin, as she did with us. We told her everything. How we walked to the pasture, that we were tanned, that we took hay to the barns. She laughed. We told her about so many things. She prayed the rosary with us and then told us that she would see us on Monday."

The apparitions were preceded by three "calls," which were described as "feelings of joy" of increasing intensity. When the children saw the Virgin, they were often in a state of ecstasy with their heads thrown back and their gazes fixed slightly above them. When this occurred, eyewitnesses reported that their bodies were so heavy that they could not be lifted; nor could the girls feel pain, either from kneeling on the rocky ground or from being stuck with needles by doctors who examined them during the apparitions.

As the apparitions continued, the girls were given objects—rosaries, medals, jewelry, and the like—for the Virgin to bless, and they astounded onlookers, and helped convince skeptics, with their ability to return them to their owners, who were previously not known to them. The girls also had an uncanny ability to recognize priests in secular dress and it was also reported that they moved with amazing speed while they were in a state of ecstasy.

In the early hours of July 1962, Conchita was the focus of a "miracle" in which the host, or communion wafer, suddenly appeared on her tongue as she kneeled "in the classical attitude of communion" in the open street by her home. The miraculous event was observed by many, because the Virgin, through Conchita, had given notice two weeks before of what has been called an "angelic administration of Communion." One of the witnesses later wrote, "the Sacred Form . . . did not give the impression of having been placed there, but rather it could be said that it blossomed with a speed superior to human eye perception"; to another, the host looked like "a snowflake upon which the sun's rays were striking." The sudden appearance of the communion wafer on the girl's tongue is known as the "little miracle" to distinguish it from the "great miracle," an event that has not yet hap-

Madonna and Angels, *detail of apse mosaic in Capella Zeno, Basilica of San Marco, Venice.*

pened, although the Virgin has revealed both the date and the nature of it to Conchita. The miracle will be visible to the Pope and to people in Garabandal, and a permanent sign of it will be left in the grove of pines where many apparitions occurred. If the great miracle does not succeed in its purpose, which is the conversion of the whole world, God's punishment will follow.

The Virgin's last message to the world at Garabandal was delivered, by the Archangel Michael to Conchita, on June 18, 1965. (By this time the other three girls had stopped seeing the Virgin.) In it, Mary expressed her displeasure at the fact that the previous message of October 18, 1961, had not been heeded. "This is the last," she warned. "Previously the cup was filling, now it is brimming over. Many priests are on the path of perdition and they take many souls with them. Today the Eucharist is given less and less importance. We should avoid the wrath of the good God on us by our good efforts."

During one of her early apparitions, the Virgin told the children that they would eventually deny the reality of the apparitions, and this prophecy eventually came true; by 1966, all four of the young women had recanted. Furthermore, the apparitions at Garabandal never received official approval; a succession of bishops and an ecclesiastical commission denied that anything of a supernatural nature had occurred at Garabandal. Still, belief in the appearances of the Virgin Mary to the four young girls there persists and is widespread. "This is the absurdity of it all," a clerical supporter wrote, "that five commissioners should be infallible, whereas thousands of others must admit to being ignorant, deluded, or, shall we say, insane." ⚭

On a Quiet Tree-Lined Street Queens, New York, 1970–Present

VERONICA LUEKEN, A MIDDLE-aged mother of five, had her first vision of the Virgin Mary on April 7, 1970. The apparition occurred in her home, a single-family residence on a quiet tree-lined street in Bayside, Queens, a borough of New York City. Mary told Mrs. Lueken that she would appear on the grounds of the nearby St. Robert Bellarmine Church on June 18, 1970. When that day came, Mary, according to Mrs.

Lueken, told her to hold prayer vigils on that site and that she wished a shrine—dedicated to Our Lady of the Roses, Mary, Help of Mothers—to be established there.

The Virgin Mary has been appearing to Veronica ever since, and Our Lady of the Roses has developed into a cult with a worldwide following, although the Catholic Church has never approved these apparitions—or any other private visions of the Virgin that have occurred in the United States in the latter part of the twentieth century. To accommodate the worshippers, the shrine has been moved nearby to the former World's Fair grounds, now Flushing Meadows–Corona Park, where on Sundays there is a Holy Hour at ten-thirty in the morning and an evening prayer vigil from eight-thirty to eleven-thirty. A message from the Virgin is received at every vigil at which Veronica is present, in recent times about once a year. The shrine calls itself the Lourdes of America because of Mary's prophecy that a "miraculous spring will erupt suddenly, like at Lourdes, to cure the ill."

According to Veronica, Jesus also appears at the vigils and speaks for a short time before Mary does. Veronica's role at these apparitions includes passing on the messages and giving a detailed, minute-by-minute description of what is happening; for example: "Now Our Lady is turning to her right and looking over. And now I see something that Our Lady has in her hand that I never noticed before during all these years of the apparitions. She has a crucifix—no, not exactly a crucifix, but a cross like mine . . ."

The Virgin's pronouncements to Veronica cover a wide range of subjects, some of them controversial political and social issues of our day. (Literature distributed by the shrine reports the Virgin's opposition to many modern trends, especially human interference with the process of conception.) Her message at Bayside is also one of impending doom. In visions, Veronica has described a threatening, comet-like body—the Ball of Redemption—that is heading toward earth. When it strikes, she warns, billions of people will die, and "man will feel that the power of the elements have [sic] shaken the very foundation of his being."

Living a life of prayer, penance, sacrifice, and church-going will help stave off the coming disaster, the Virgin has told Veronica. The pious should received the Eucharist "daily if

possible," pray the rosary, read the Bible but only "editions published before 1964," wear the brown scapular and other sacramentals, and "spread the Message of Heaven, and, above all, await the return of Christ to earth, which will be soon." ⁌

HANDMAIDEN OF THE EUCHARIST
AKITA, JAPAN, 1973

SISTER AGNES KATSUKO SASAGAWA had only been at the convent at Akita in northern Japan for a month when she perceived a bright light coming from the tabernacle. The phenomenon, which first occurred on June 12, 1973, was repeated several times over the following weeks. During this time she was also visited by her guardian angel, "a person covered with shining whiteness like snow." Sister Agnes was forty-two years old and stone deaf.

On June 28, a small wound shaped like a cross appeared on her left palm; it was accompanied by excruciating pain. A week later the wound began to bleed. Early in the morning of the next day (July 6), her guardian angel appeared again and told her: "The wounds of Mary are much deeper and more sorrowful than yours." He accompanied her to the chapel to pray, then disappeared.

Alone in the chapel, Sister Agnes approached a small statue of Mary, only twenty-seven and a half inches high, that had been carved by a Buddhist sculptor in 1965. Suddenly a brilliant light radiated from the statue and, Sister Agnes later recounted, "a voice of indescribable beauty struck my totally deaf ears." The voice addressed her as "my daughter" and told her that her deafness would be cured and that the pain in her hand was to remind her to pray for mankind. Her guardian angel then reappeared and joined in the recitation of a prayer of the convent, which is called the Institute of the Handmaids of the Holy Eucharist. The prayer begins: "O Jesus, truly present in the Host and offered in sacrifice at each moment on all the altars on earth . . ." (The word "truly" was added to the prayer on the instructions of the voice, which, by now, Sister Agnes took to be that of the Virgin Mary.)

The next morning blood was discovered flowing from a small cross-shaped wound in the hand of the statue that was identical in its configuration to Sister Agnes's wound and was

Betye Saar (b. 1926), Pájaro–Bird Reliquary, 1989, collection of the artist.

so realistic that it appeared to be flesh instead of wood. On July 27, as her guardian angel had promised, Sister Agnes's wound disappeared. On August 3, she again heard the statue speak, warning this time of "a great chastisement" that God is preparing to inflict on mankind. The wound vanished from the statue's hand on September 29; the same day the sisters saw a brilliant light radiating from the statue, which appeared covered with moisture as if it were perspiring. Some sisters dried the statue with cotton swabs.

Sister Agnes heard the final message from the statue of Mary on October 13, the anniversary of the day the sun danced at Fátima, Portugal. "If men do not repent," the voice warned, there will be a punishment "greater than the deluge, such as one will never have seen before. Fire will fall from the sky . . ." The message ended with a command: "Pray very much the prayers of the Rosary. I alone am able still to save you from the calamities which approach. Those who place their confidence in me will be saved."

It was the last message from the statue to Sister Agnes, but the miracles of Akita were not over. On January 4, 1979, the statue wept, and it continued to weep, off and on, 101 times between that day and September 15, 1981. Two weeks after the tears ceased, Sister Agnes's guardian angel appeared to her for the last time and showed her a Bible open to God's words to the serpent in Genesis 3:15: "I shall put enmity between thee and the woman, and between thy seed and her seed . . ."

The angel also explained the significance of the number 101, the times the statue shed tears: the two 1's represent, first, Eve, who brought sin into the world, and then Mary "through whom evil had been overcome." The zero between them "signifies the Eternal God Who is from all eternity until eternity."

Samples of the tears—and the blood and perspiration—were analyzed and determined to be of human origin. On May 30, 1982, Sister Agnes was permanently cured of her deafness, a condition that had been considered incurable. In 1984, Bishop John Shojiro Ito of the Diocese of Niigata authorized "the veneration of the Holy Mother of Akita." In the same pastoral letter he added this assessment of Sister Agnes, whom he had known for ten years: "She is a woman sound in spirit, frank and without problems. . . . Consequently the messages she says that she has received did not appear to me to be in any way the result of imagination or hallucination." ❧

Russian icon (12th century), Madonna and Child, *San Francesca Romana, Rome.*

Picture Credits and Annotations

COVER Peruvian, 18th century, Collao School, *Virgin of the Assumption.* Private collection, Venice. Photo: Claudio Franzini. Executed with fine attention to detail, this work by an anonymous master was created at Collao, north of Lima, one of the artistic centers that flourished in colonial Peru during the seventeenth and eighteenth centuries.

1 Serbian Orthodox, mid-18th century, *Madonna and Child,* Galerija Matice Srpske, Novi Sad, Serbia. Erich Lessing/Art Resource, NY. This formal and hieratic devotional image is typical of the Eastern tradition of idealized, iconic interpretations of Mary, paintings intended specifically for veneration.

TITLE PAGE Sandro Botticelli (1455–1510), *Madonna of the Magnificat.* Tempera on wood, 46 ½ in. (118 cm.) diameter. Uffizi Gallery, Florence. Scala/Art Resource, NY. This Italian Renaissance masterpiece takes its name from the book open to a page with the "Magnificat" inscribed.

5 Johann Eckhard Löffler and Heinrich Löffler, *Felicite Me Floribus Quia Amore Langueo.* Engraving from *Flores seraphici sive icones vitae et gesta via ovum illustrium,* Cologne, 1640–42. Spencer Collection, The New York Public Library; Astor, Lenox and Tilden Foundations. Photo: Robert D. Rubic, New York City. This work and several others that follow are from an early printed book of devotional images produced in Cologne during the Counterreformation, when the cult of Mary had received new impetus and was flourishing.

1 OUR LADY OF PEACE AND PRAYER

12 Abbott Handerson Thayer (1849–1921), *The Virgin.* Oil on canvas, 90½ x 72 in. (229.7 x 182.5 cm.). Courtesy of the Freer Gallery of Art, Smithsonian Institution, Washington. D.C. 93.11. As a late-nineteenth-century Romantic Idealist, Thayer portrayed the Virgin as a young American girl, striding ahead purposefully; he may have used his own daughter Mary as his model.

15 Arroyo Hondo Santero, *Our Lady of Sorrows/ Nuestra Señora de los Delores,* 1830/40. Santos figure, 25 in. (62.2 cm.). Private collection. Photo: Michael O'Shaugnessy from *New Kingdom of the Saints—Religious Art of New Mexico 1780–1907* by Larry Frank, published by Red Crane Books, Santa Fe, NM. The angular forms and mask-like facial features of this carved statue are typical of santos figures from the American Southwest.

16 Jacopo Ligozzi (1547–1627), *The Beech Tree of the Madonna at La Verna.* Pen and brown wash over black chalk, 15⅞ x 10⅛ in. (40.2 x 25.7 cm.). Metropolitan Museum of Art, The Harry G. Sperling Fund, 1983 (1983.131.1). The late Renaissance artist's keen observation of the natural world resulted in a beautiful rendering of a lush forested landscape. Ligozzi is also known for his botanical drawings.

19 Nicolas Poussin (1594–1665), *The Assumption of the Virgin,* c. 1626. Oil on canvas, 53 x 38½ in. (1.344 x .981 m.). Ailsa Mellon Bruce Fund, © 1995 Board of Trustees, National Gallery of Art, Washington, D.C. 1963.5.1 (1905)/PA. This is a detail from a larger painting by the French Baroque painter Poussin that included two monumental classical columns.

23 German, Middle Rhine, attributed to the Master of the Amsterdam Cabinet, *Virgin of the Apocalypse,* 1480/90. Glass — stained, 13⅞ x 9⅝ in. (35.2 x 24.4 cm.). The Metropolitan

Museum of Art, The Cloisters Collection, 1982 (1982.47.1). All rights reserved, The Metropolitan Museum of Art. The jewel-like medium of stained glass here contains a Virgin-and-Child image similar to that seen in German engravings of the same period.

24 Johann Eckhard Löffler and Heinrich Löffler, *F. Leo Catanensis Laicus.* Engraving (detail) from *Flores seraphici sive icones vitae et gesta via ovum illustrium,* Cologne, 1640–42. Spencer Collection, The New York Public Library; Astor, Lenox and Tilden Foundations. Photo: Robert D. Rubic, New York City. See page 5, above.

26-27 Titian (Tiziano Vecelli; c. 1488–1576), *The Virgin with the Rabbit,* 1530. 28 x 34¼ in. (71 x 87 cm.). Musée du Louvre. © Réunion des Musées Nationaux. The Venetian Renaissance master Titian, known for his limpid colors and delicately rendered figures, painted this endearing image for a princely patron, Federigo Gonzaga, who may be portrayed in the scene as a shepherd.

29 Swabia, *Mary in a Robe Embroidered with Ears of Corn (Maria im Ährenkleid),* 1450/60, Woodcut. Staatliche Graphische Sammlung, Munich. Mary is here shown dressed in a gown decorated with ears of corn or wheat, traditional symbols of the harvest and abundance.

2 HEALING MARY

30 Jacopo Pontormo (1494–1556), *The Visitation.* San Michele, Carmignano, Italy. Scala/Art Resource, NY. The story of Mary's meeting with Elizabeth, mother of John the Baptist, before either woman had given birth, is shown in this monumental image by the Florentine painter: his palette of acid greens and oranges and his disregard for an accurate rendering of the human figure mark this as a Mannerist work.

34 Bartolomé Esteban Murillo (1617–1682), *The Soult Immaculate Conception,* c. 1678. Museo del Prado. © Museo del Prado,

Madrid, all rights reserved. Total or partial reproduction is prohibited. Born in Seville and one of the founders of the Seville Academy, the Spanish Baroque painter Murillo here creates an intensely devotional work.

37 Jesús Guerrero Galván (1910–1973), *Madonna and Child,* 1946. Oil on canvas, 28 x 22.5 in. (77.1 x 57.9 cm.). Photograph courtesy of Mary-Anne Martin/Fine Art, New York City. The Mexican twentieth-century painter Galván draws on the modern European styles of Cubism as well as on the classicism of antiquity and the dynamic sculptural styles of ancient Mexico for his pensive depiction of the Madonna and Child.

39 Joseph Stella (1877–1946), *The Virgin,* 1926. Oil on canvas, 39⅝ x 38¾ in. (100.5 x 98.4 cm.). The Brooklyn Museum 28.207. Gift of Adolph Lewisohn. Here an introspective Mary by the Italian-American painter is surrounded by a virtual cornucopia of fruits, flowers, and birds; even her mantle is patterned with flowers and trailing vines.

41 Leonardo da Vinci (1452–1519), *The Virgin and Child with St. Anne.* 66¼ x 51¼ in. (168 x 130 cm.). Musée du Louvre, © Réunion des Musées Nationaux. A masterpiece of Western painting, Leonardo's intimate portrayal of the Virgin, her Son, and her mother is a landmark in the history of art for its structured, pyramidal composition.

43 Johann Eckhard Löffler and Heinrich Löffler, *F. Bernardinus a Murciano Laicus.* Engraving (detail) from volume 1, p. 45 of *Flores seraphici sive icones vitae et gesta via ovum illustrium,* Cologne, 1640–42. Spencer Collection, The New York Public Library; Astor, Lenox and Tilden Foundations. Photo: Robert D. Rubic, New York City. See page 5, above.

44 Caravaggio, Michelangelo Merisi da (1571–1610), *Madonna of the Pilgrims.* San Agostino, Rome. Scala/Art Resource, NY. Here the Roman Baroque painter builds a composition of intersecting horizontals, verticals, and diagonals to create a dynamic image of Mary and Jesus adored by pilgrims.

47 Mexican, *Ex-voto of Dolores Hernandez,* 1938. Ex-voto, 11⅞ x 16½ in. (30.1 x 41.8 cm.). Private collection. Photo: Tim Fuller, Tucson, AZ. In this image offering thanks to Mary for her intercession in saving an ill daughter, the detailed interior scene offers a rare glimpse of upper-class life in Mexico in the 1930s: the sick room features items then considered luxurious, such as paintings and lace curtains.

3 SILENT MARY

48 Mexican, 19th century, *Madonna on a Crescent Moon.* Feather art. Staatliche Museen zu Berlin, Museum für Völkerkunde. Feathers traditionally were used in the ceremonial and funerary art of such ancient civilizations as the Aztec in Mexico and the Inca in Peru. Here Mary, Queen of Heaven, is rendered in this unusual medium.

51 Vittore Carpaccio (c. 1460/5–1523/6), *Virgin Reading,* c. 1505. Oil on panel transferred to canvas, 30¾ x 20 in. (78.1 x 50.6 cm.). Samuel H. Kress Collection, © 1995 Board of Trustees, National Gallery of Art, Washington, D.C. 1939.1.354 (447)/PA. This painting, a fragment of a larger, narrative composition by the Venetian Renaissance artist, may have originally included the Christ Child at play.

52 Master Francke (active c. 1405–after 1424), *Nativity,* from the Englandfahrer Altarpiece. 39 x 35 in. Hamburger Kunsthalle, Hamburg. This quiet scene, representing the birth of Christ, is from a much larger work that the Rhenish master created for a company of Hamburg merchants who traded with England.

54 Jean Fouquet (c. 1420–1481), *Mary and Jesus Surrounded by Seraphim and Cherubim* (right half of the Melun Diptych), c. 1450. 36¾ x 27¼ in. (94.5 x 85.5 cm.). Koninklijk Museum voor Schone Kunsten, Antwerp,

Belgium. This representation of the Virgin enthroned was commissioned by Etienne Chevalier, treasurer to Charles VII of France. It portrays Agnès Sorel, court beauty and mistress to the king, as the Madonna.

57 Geertgen tot Sint Jans (c.1455/65–1485/95), *Night Nativity,* c. 1485/95. Reproduced by courtesy of the Trustees, The National Gallery, London. In this solemn depiction of the birth of Christ, the tiny body of the Christ Child serves to illuminate the scene, emanating an unearthly light unrivaled by either the shepherds' campfire or the angel announcing the birth above.

58 School of Dijon (early 15th century), *Virgin and Child.* Musée du Louvre, © Réunion des Musées Nationaux. The sinuous elegance of the figures and gold ground are evidence of the Late Gothic style of this anonymous master.

62·63 Henry Ossawa Tanner (1859–1937), *The Annunciation,* 1898. Oil on canvas, 57 x 71¼ in. (144.8 x 180.9 cm.). Philadelphia Museum of Art: W. P. Wilstach Collection (W' 99-1-1). After receiving his artistic training in Philadelphia, the African-American artist moved to Paris where his work won critical acclaim. He completed this impressive work on his return from a sojourn to the Holy Land in 1897 and exhibited it in Paris at the 1898 salon.

4 MARY OF SAINTS

64 Piero di Cosimo (c. 1462–1521?), *Immaculate Conception with Six Saints.* Oil on wood, 81⅛ x 67¾ in. (206 x 172 cm.). Uffizi Gallery, Florence. Erich Lessing/Art Resource, NY. This carefully structured composition was painted for a chapel in the church of Santissima Annunziata, Florence.

67 Gondar, Ethiopia, after 1730, *Our Lady Mary at Dabra Metmaq.* Tempera on gesso-covered wood panels, 14⅜ x 12¾ (36.2 x 32.3 cm.). Institute of Ethiopian Studies, Addis Ababa, no. 4144. Photo: Malcolm Varon,

New York City, © 1995. This triptych presents the miraculous appearance of Mary at Dabra Metmaq. A strong devotion to Mary is part of the Ethiopian Christian tradition.

70 Sano di Pietro (1406–1481), *Madonna Appearing to Pope Callistus III.* Pinacoteca Nazionale, Siena. Scala/Art Resource, NY. This version of the Virgin appearing to Pope Callistus III is set in a picturesque landscape outside the walls of a medieval city, perhaps the artist's native Siena. Pope Callistus III was responsible for reopening the trial of Joan of Arc, twenty-three years after she was executed for heresy.

73 Francisco de Zurbarán (1598–1664), *The Young Virgin,* c. 1635/40. Oil on canvas, 46 x 37 in. (116.8 x 94 cm.). The Metropolitan Museum of Art, Fletcher Fund, 1927 (27.137). The Spanish Baroque painter here represents Mary as a serious and devout young girl. According to medieval legend she spent her days in prayer, sewing vestments, while she lived at the Temple in Jerusalem.

75 Pedro Berruguete (1450–1503/4), *Virgin Appearing to a Community of Dominicans,* c. 1490/99. Museo del Prado. © Museo del Prado, Madrid, all rights reserved. Total or partial reproduction is prohibited. Berruguete trained as an artist in his native Spain and became court painter to Ferdinand and Isabella.

76 Andrea Mantegna (c. 1431–1506), *Madonna with Child and Saints.* Galleria Sabauda, Turin. Scala/Art Resource, NY. Mantegna's rendering of the figures emphasizes their solid, geometric character and reflects his interest in the forms of classical antiquity.

79 Jusepe Ribera (1591?–1652), *The Holy Family with Saints Anne and Catherine of Alexandria,* 1648. Oil on canvas, 82½ x 60¾ in. (209.6 x 154.3 cm.). Metropolitan Museum of Art, Samuel D. Lee Fund, 1934 (34.73). A Spanish artist, Ribera worked mainly in Italy where he absorbed the lessons of Italian Baroque style.

5 OUR LADY OF SORROW

80 El Greco (Domenikos Theotocopoulos; 1541–1614), *Mater Dolorosa,* c. 1585. Oil on canvas, 26½ x 20½ in. (63 x 48 cm.). Thyssen-Bornemisza Collection, Lugano. Known for his ecstatic, passionate style of painting, El Greco here evokes the emotional agitation beneath the smooth surface of Mary's mournful face through his brushwork for her mantle and gown.

85 Cruz López (b. 1974), *Our Lady of Sorrows/Nuestra Señora de los Dolores.* Santos figure. Maxwell Museum of Anthropology, Albuquerque, NM. A contemporary artist active in New Mexico, Cruz López looks to both traditional arts of the Southwest as well as Western art for his inspiration. In carving this moving image, the young artist has said: "My experience was very spiritual. . . . I could feel some of the sorrow that Mary had when Christ died."

87 Peruvian, 18th century, Cuzco School, *Our Lady of Sorrows/Nuestra Señora de los Dolores.* Private collection, Venice. Photo: Claudio Franzini. Cuzco, the royal city of the Inca, was an important artistic center in colonial Peru through the eighteenth century, and a place where the old and new civilizations coexisted. The Indian style and popular traditions contributed to a unique school of painting.

89 Mexican, late 19th century, *Sorrowful Mary.* Retablo. Private collection. Photo: Tim Fuller, Tucson, AZ. This work on tin is a devotional painting by an anonymous nineteenth-century Mexican artist.

91 Geertgen tot Sint Jans (c. 1455/65–1485/95), detail from *Man of Sorrows.* Museum Catharijneconvent, Utrecht. This deeply poignant image of Mary is a detail from a larger narrative work in which she contemplates her wounded Son, crowned with thorns and carrying His cross.

6 "BUILD ME HERE A CHURCH"

92 Giovanni-Antonio Badile (1516/17–1562), *Madonna and Child*. Santa Maria Ala Scala, Verona. SuperStock. Here the Madonna and Child are enthroned on an elaborate chair that has the architectural characteristics of a Gothic cathedral, a reminder of the origins of the cathedral structure itself as *cathedra*, the seat of Christendom.

96-97 Bartolomé Estebán Murillo (1617–1682), *The Foundation of Santa Maria Maggiore in Rome: The Patrician's Dream*, c. 1662/65. Museo del Prado. © Museo del Prado, Madrid, all rights reserved. Total or partial reproduction is prohibited. See page 34, above.

100 Master of the Saint Lucy Legend (active 1480–1489), *Mary, Queen of Heaven*, c. 1485. Oil on wood panel, 78½ x 63¾ in. (2.015 x 1.638 m.). Samuel H. Kress Collection, © 1995 Board of Trustees, National Gallery of Art, Washington, D.C. 1952.2.13. (1096)/PA. This unusual picture by an early Netherlandish master combines several aspects of Marian devotion in one scene: the Immaculate Conception, the Assumption, and the Coronation of the Virgin.

103 José Rafael Aragón (active 1820–1862), *Virgin of Guadalupe*, c. 1830s. Santos figure. 83 x 34.9 cm. Private collection. Photo: Michael O'Shaugnessy from *New Kingdom of the Saints—Religious Art of New Mexico 1780–1907* by Larry Frank, published by Red Crane Books, Santa Fe, NM.

104 Rufino Tamayo (1899–1991), *The Virgin of Guadalupe*, 1926. Gouache on paper, 10 x 6¾ in. (25.4 x 17.1 cm.). Photograph courtesy of Mary-Anne Martin/Fine Art, New York City. Tamayo, a Mexican artist, drew on pre-Columbian traditions as well as on modern European art.

108 Gentile da Fabriano (1370–1427), *Coronation of the Virgin*, c. 1420s. Collection of the J. Paul Getty Museum, Malibu, California. A master of the International Gothic style, Gentile da Fabriano employs textile patterns, jewel-like colors, and embossed gold in this compelling work.

111 Luis Niño (active c. 1730–1750), *Our Lady of the Victory of Málaga*, c. 1735. Potosí school. Oil and gold on canvas, 59½ x 50½ in. (151 x 128.2 cm.). Denver Art Museum, 1969.345. The Indian artist Niño worked in Potosí, an important artistic center in colonial Peru.

7 LADY OF THE HELPING HAND

112 Canadian, 18th century, *Ex-voto of Monsieur Roger*, 1717. Oil on canvas, 99 x 74 in. (246 x 188 cm.). Basilique Sainte-Anne-de-Beaupré, Quebec. This appealing votive painting was commissioned by a Quebec merchant. Mary and her mother Anne are invoked to aid a ship caught in the ice as men abandon the doomed vessel. One figure, still on board, prays fervently.

115 Ethiopian, after 1600, *Our Lady Mary with Her Beloved Son* (triptych, center panel). Tempera on gesso-covered wood panels, 20 x 18¾ in. (51 x 50 cm.). Institute of Ethiopian Studies, Addis Ababa, no. 4261. Photo: Malcolm Varon, New York City, © 1995. Mary is shown with her son and flanked by archangels.

116 Polish, 17th century, *Virgin of Czechtochowa*. Engraving from *Obsidio clari montis Czestochoviensis* by Stanislaus Kobierzycki, Danzig, 1659. Rare Books and Manuscripts Division, The New York Public Library, Astor, Lenox and Tilden Foundations. Photo: Robert D. Rubic, NYC. This engraving is from a printed book chronicling the miracle-working icon beloved by Polish Catholics.

118-119 Giovanni Antonio Vanoni (1810–1886), *Ex-voto from the Oratory of the "Poss," Golino*,

Switzerland. Tempera on canvas, 22½ x 28¾ in. (57 x 73 cm.). Ufficio dei Musei Etnografici, Giubiasco, Switzerland. The votive painting by this Swiss artist shows the Madonna interceding on behalf of an accident victim; in the distance is a spectacular scene of the city of Golino and snow-topped Alps.

123 Sandro Botticelli (1445–1510), *The Annunciation* (detail). 59 x 61½ in. (150 x 156 cm.). Uffizi Gallery, Florence. Erich Lessing/ Art Resource, NY. This is a detail from a larger work that was commissioned from the Florentine painter in 1489.

125 English, 12th century, *Virgin and Child.* Manuscript illumination. Bodleian Library, Oxford. MS. Bodl. 269, fol. iiir. This manuscript page exemplifies the Romanesque style.

8 Mary's Gifts

126 Mario Parial (Philippines, b. 1945), *Our Lady of Mt. Carmel/Nuestra Señora del Carmen.* Acrylic on canvas, 48 x 32 in. (121.9 x 81.3 cm.). Dr. and Mrs. Yolando Sulit Collection. From *Art Philippines,* © 1992 by the Crucible Workshop, Manila. Photo: Dick Baldovino. Basing his art on the folk traditions of his native Philippines, Parial, like some of his contemporaries, consciously rejects the urban aesthetic advocated in the capital Manila.

129 Caravaggio, Michelangelo Merisi da (1571–1610), *Madonna of the Rosary with Saint Dominic and Saint Peter Martyr,* 1607. Oil on canvas, 143⅜ x 98 in. (364 x 249 cm.). Kunsthistorisches Museum, Vienna. Erich Lessing/ Art Resource, NY. The power of this scene, which exemplifies Roman Baroque style, is underscored by stark light and deep shadows.

130 Mexican, late 19th century, *Our Lady of Mt. Carmel/Nuestra Señora de Carmen.* Retablo. 7 x 10 in. (17.8 x 25.4 cm.). Private collection. Photo: Tim Fuller, Tucson, AZ. Here Mary and the Christ Child hold scapulars resembling those of the Carmelite Order.

132 "De Beatissimo B. Mariae Virginis Sacello Laurentano." Engraving from *Vita Beatae Mariae Virginis,* Cologne, 1592. Spencer Collection, The New York Public Library; Astor, Lenox and Tilden Foundations. The life of the Virgin was a popular subject from the earliest days of printing. The centralized image reflects Renaissance compositional style.

135 Mexican, late 19th century, *Our Lady of the Holy Cave/Nuestra Señora de la Cueva Santa.* Retablo, 4 x 6¼ in. (10.1 x 15.8 cm.). Private collection. Photo: Tim Fuller, Tucson, AZ. A few lines suffice to define the Virgin's features in this poignant folk image.

137 Johann Eckhard Löffler and Heinrich Löffler, *Fr. Constantinus a Patricio Laicus,* Engraving (detail) from volume 2, p. 30 of *Flores seraphici sive icones vitae et gesta via ovum illustrium,* Cologne, 1640–42. Spencer Collection, The New York Public Library; Astor, Lenox and Tilden Foundations. Photo: Robert D. Rubic, New York City. See page 5, above.

139 Fernando Aguilár (19th century), *Virgin of the Light with Saint Joseph, Saint Michael the Archangel, Saint John Nepomucene, and Saint Anthony/Virgen de la Luz con San José, el Arcángel San Miguel, San Juan Nepomuceno y San Antonio.* 28⅜ x 21¾ in. (72 x 55 cm.). Museo Franz Mayer, Mexico City. The image of the Virgin of the Light, venerated in Spain, had its origins in the seventeenth century. This specific image is a highly stylized and dramatic interpretation.

142-143 Elena Climent (b. 1955), *Altar with Photographs and Candles/ Altar con fotografías y veladores,* 1993. Oil on canvas mounted on Masonite, 18¼ x 23½ in. (46 x 59.5 cm.). Photograph courtesy of Mary-Anne Martin/Fine Art, New York City. A Mexican artist living and working in New York, Climent portrays the personal, everyday objects of her countrymen today.

9 LADY OF LEGEND

146 Nahum B. Zenil (b. 1947), *Benediciones/ Blessings,* 1990. Mixed media on paper, 20¼ x 14¾ in. (51.5 x 37.5 cm.). Collection of Sra. Yolanda Santos de Garza Lagüera, Monterrey, Mexico. Photo courtesy of The Americas Society, New York City. A contemporary Mexican artist, Zenil works with traditional themes and imagery but frequently makes use of them to challenge accepted social and political notions.

150 Piero della Francesca (1410/20–1492), *Madonna del Parto.* Chapel of the Cemetery, Monterchi, Italy. Scala/Art Resource, NY. This painting, by one of the great masters of the Italian Renaissance, is to be found in a small cemetary chapel near the artist's native Borgo San Sepolchro.

154 English or French School (?), *Richard II Presented to the Virgin and Child* (right half of the Wilton Diptych), c. 1395. Reproduced by courtesy of the Trustees, The National Gallery, London. This rare example of early English painting may have been made as a Crusader icon to commemorate Richard II's vow to make a crusade to the Holy Land with France's Charles VI.

158 Lower Bavaria (Pilgramsberg), *In Gratitude to the Virgin,* 1882. Votive painting, oil on wood, 12⅝ x 6¾ in. (32.3 x 17.1 cm.). Bavarian National Museum, Munich. Votive paintings such as this traditionally present a mix of religion and popular culture.

161 Peruvian, late 18th century, Cuzco School, *Nursing Madonna.* Oil on linen, 32 x 26½ in. (81.3 x 67.3 cm.). New Orleans Museum of Art #74.266. Symbolic elements such as the grapes of the Holy Eucharist and strawberries, emblems of Mary's moral perfection, are carefully presented in this colonial Peruvian work.

10 MARY'S WARNINGS

162 Odilon Redon (1840–1916), *Virgin of the Dawn,* 1890. Oil on canvas, 21 x 14½ in. (53.5 x 37 cm.). Collection of Mr. and Mrs. Robert Donnelley. Photograph courtesy of The Art Institute of Chicago. Redon's dreamlike, fantastic images from the late nineteenth century identify him as a leading Symbolist painter.

167 Geertgen tot Sint Jans (1455/65– 1485/95), *The Glorification of the Virgin,* 10½ x 8 in. (26.8 x 20.5 cm.). Museum Boymans-van Beuningen, Rotterdam. This Dutch artist produced a number of powerful religious works before his early death at age 28.

171 Giambattista Tiepolo (1696–1770), *The Immaculate Conception,* 1769. Museo del Prado. © Museo del Prado, Madrid, all rights reserved. Total or partial reproduction is prohibited. This image was one of seven large canvases executed for the church of San Pascual de Aranjuez in Madrid.

173 *Madonna and Angels.* Detail of apse in Capella Zeno. Byzantine mosaic, basilica of San Marco, Venice. Scala/Art Resource, NY. In the fourth century, the center of Christendom was moved from Rome to Constantinople and from there, the Byzantine style emerged.

176 Betye Saar (b. 1926), *Pájaro—Bird Reliquary,* 1989. Mixed media assemblage, 11¼ x 6½ x 2 in. (28.5 x 16.5 x 5 cm.). Collection of the artist. Photo: William Nettles. A contemporary African-American artist, Saar draws on ceremonial traditions from cultures such as Africa and South America for her art.

179 Russian icon, 12th century, *Madonna and Child.* San Francesca Romana, Rome. Scala/Art Resource, NY. Byzantine style remained a strong tradition in Eastern Christendom, reaching a high point in the late Middle Ages.

Books about Mary

Although the subject of *Miracles of Mary* is spiritual, the sources of information are very much of this world, namely, a variety of works, both devotional and scholarly, on Marian apparitions and miracles. Those that were most valuable in compiling this book are mentioned here.

Foremost among devotional works, which treat miracles as opportunities to enhance Marian devotion, are the four volumes, *The Apparitions and Shrines of Heaven's Bright Queen,* which William J. Walsh published in 1904. Walsh is delightfully indiscriminating about miracles; an apparition of the early Christian era is as real to him as one occurring in his own lifetime. His accounts are invaluable for their details, many of which found their way into this book.

Although he wrote a half-century later, H. M. Gillett is in the same tradition; his 1949 work, *Famous Shrines of Our Lady,* was particularly helpful. A 1960 book edited by John J. Delaney, *A Woman Clothed with the Sun: Eight Great Appearances of Our Lady in Modern Times,* consists of well-researched accounts by different Catholic experts. The entries are good examples of devotional writing brought up to date. Joan Carroll Cruz has written a handy guide, *Miraculous Images of Our Lady: 100 Famous Catholic Portraits and Statues* (1993). Joan Ashton's *Mother of All Nations* (1989) contains accounts of Marian visitations throughout history.

Scholarly literature concentrates on what apparitions and miracles reveal about the times in which they occurred. The quality in this field is uneven, a mixture of the mediocre with the superb. Some of the best books, such as Sandra Zimdars-Swartz's *Encountering Mary: From La Salette to Medjugorje* (1991), are published by Princeton University Press, which seems to have made Marian apparitions a subspecialty. Princeton has also published four books on Spanish religious phenomena by William A. Christian, including his *Apparitions in Late Medieval and Renaissance Spain* (1981). In his *The Cult of the Virgin Mary: Psychological Origins* (also Princeton, 1986), Michael P. Carroll includes interesting details about important apparitions while arguing that their origins are either hallucinatory or illusionary. In 1994, a Harvard professor, David Blackbourn, published *Marpingen: Apparitions of the Virgin Mary in Bismarckian Germany,* a thoroughly researched and detailed account of how a sequence of apparitions became politicized.

Finally, among all books, I found Marina Warner's *Alone of All Her Sex: The Myth and the Cult of the Virgin Mary* (1976) to be outstanding—informative, readable, witty at times, and provocative.

—M.D.

Acknowledgments

THE PROJECT STAFF IS GRATEFUL to the many people who contributed advice, time, expertise, and sometimes even supplies to the making of this book. Just a few names are below, but to everyone—named and unnamed—our heartfelt thanks is extended.

The staff for this project must permit itself a pat on the back: a more talented group of people could not have been at work than Kevin Callahan, Moira Duggan, Gail Reichstein, and Elizabeth Stoneman, with additional contributions from researchers Amy Wilensky and Sloan Seiden, writer Lorraine Karafel, indexer Pat Woodruff, and proofreaders Wendy Fisher and Kathy Talalay.

The evolution of the visual concept for the book was helped along at various stages by Lauren Stransky, Frank Nappi, James Zihal, Erle Grubb, David Trieger, Michael Romanski, and the Francis J. Zaino Family focus group.

Curators, museum administrators, collectors, galleries, artists, and other publishers were extremely generous in their advice about how to find unusual images of the Virgin Mary and sometimes went to great lengths to have transparencies made for us. Even if we were not ultimately able to use images you helped us find, thank you all, especially: Guillermo J. Andrade, Jacklyn Burns at the Getty, William R. Calhoun at The Maxwell Museum, Melissa Dalziel, Caroline Demaree, Francine Dion of the Basilique de Sainte-Anne-de-Beaupré, Robert Donnelley, Elizabeth K. Fonseca, Gloria Fraser Giffords, Adam Jolles, Denise Klingman, LaVita Emory of the Freer Gallery of Art, Elizabeth Ferrer of the Americas Society, Augusto Gaggioni, Dr. Nina Gockerell of the Bavarian National Museum, Heidrun Klein, Felix Liddell of Livre Noir, Catherine Malone of the Santa Barbara Museum of Art, Mary-Ann Martin of Mary-Ann Martin/Fine Art in New York, Rene Luis S. Mata, Roswitha Neu-Kock, Dr. Marian Oettinger of the San Antonio Museum of Art, Michael O'Shaughnessy of Red Crane Books, Ruth Roa at The Crucible Workshop in Manila, Linda Raymonds of the British Library, Matthew Rembe at Mary-Ann Martin/Fine Art, Susan Rossen, Betye Saar, Kees van Schooten, Sarah Sibbald, Abby Sider of the Americas Society, Joanne Stuhr of the Tucson Museum of Art, Prof. Edward Sullivan, Georg Syamken, David Witt at the Harwood Foundation, Malcolm Varon, Joseph R. Wolin of the Americas Society, Alejandra R. de Yturbe of Galeria de Arte Mexicano, Nahum Zenil.

Others who contributed advice, skills, and various forms of moral support include Dr. David L. Green, Patricia A. Graney, Sr. Elizabeth Johnson, Brigitte Graney, and Lois Turel.

This entire project could not have been possible without the support and enthusiasm of our editor, Kevin Bentley, whose professionalism and clear thinking helped us every step of the way. Many thanks to Kevin and the entire team at HarperSanFrancisco.

Index

Italicized page numbers refer to illustrations